VAUXHALL

ADVANC

DRIVING

GORDON COLE

LONDON

IAN ALLAN LTD

Acknowledgements

First published 1986
Third impression 1990

ISBN 0 7110 1643 7

Published by Ian Allan Ltd,
Shepperton, Surrey; and printed
by Ian Allan Printing Ltd at their
works at Coombelands in
Runnymede, England

I thank my friends most sincerely for the time and patience
necessary to arrange the photographs.

The drivers were: Irene Bradon, Barbara Young, Maureen
Cooper, Allan Murrey and Bob Stewart. Very special thanks go
to George Carruthers and Ted Teer, both ex-Advanced Driving
Instructors of The Metropolitan Police Motor Driving School,
Hendon, and Joint Senior Examiners of ROSPA Advanced
Drivers' Association.

References and extracts are from:
Highways Economic Note No 1, The Cost of Road Accidents 1982
and *Roadcraft* (material is reproduced with the permission
of the Controller of Her Majesty's Stationery Office).
Motorways by James Drake, published by Faber & Faber.
Moriarty's Police Law, published by Butterworth.
Harrow Observer, Harrow.
*The History of The Metropolitan Police Motor Driving School,
Hendon*, by Bill Fleming.
Accident statistics
Supplied by RoSPA.

Drinking and driving
Statistics courtesy of the Home Office.

All photography was by the author using a Rolleiflex 6006
camera with Carl Zeiss lenses, supplied by AV Distributors
(London) Ltd (Tel 01-226 1508).

Historical and Police Driving Schools photographs supplied by
the Publicity Department, Metropolitan Police, New Scotland
Yard, London.

A special thank you to Vauxhall Motors, Luton, which so kindly
supplied the vehicles.

Damaged vehicles were supplied by Universal Salvage Ltd,
Redbourn, Herts.

Developing and printing by Kingsley Michael, Letchworth.

Most of all, however, I'd like to thank those members of the
general public who — unwittingly — helped make the
pre-arranged traffic situations more realistic for me.

Gordon Cole

Contents

1 Advanced Driving

Most of us have seen a road accident at one time or another: we know how it happened, but not always why. It only takes one thoughtless driver, cyclist or pedestrian to cause a lot of pain, suffering and damage to property.

The motor car has been designed to start, stop, go forwards, backwards, turn left and right. This must be done in complete safety, creating no inconvenience or danger to any other road user or pedestrian while travelling in whatever direction. However, accident statistics over many years inform us that over 5,000 people are killed on our roads each year. What a waste of life and money this figure represents.

The new enthusiasm for Advanced Driving is encouraging, not only because of the personal gain in financial and pleasurable benefits which can be derived from having the ability to drive to the high standard required to pass the Advanced Driving Test, but because of the satisfaction that a person can prove, by examination, that he or she is a safer and more competent driver than their next door neighbour or colleague at work.

There are three factors which can cause a road accident: human error, mechanical failure and the environment. In some accidents two factors are the cause, but very rarely do three interact. Statistics have proved that in nine times out of 10, the causation factor can be traced to human error. Of course, road accidents happen in all types of weather, on all types of road, at all times of the day and night.

It is of the utmost importance that a driver has a thorough understanding of the workings of an engine and transmission system. This knowledge, combined with intelligent use of the accelerator, clutch, gears and brakes, will enable the driver to change gear with smoothness and in complete safety, with minimum wear to the vehicle. This consideration for the vehicle is the hallmark of an expert professional driver, who will gain maximum efficiency from the engine, and in return will achieve economical motoring, which is part of the ultimate aim of Advanced Driving. A driver with a good understanding of the controls of his vehicle, who drives smoothly and unobtrusively, who is alert but looks relaxed, who knows the capabilities and handling characteristics of his vehicle, who combines these with good powers of concentration, observation, anticipation and patience, will recognise potential danger well in advance and act on what is seen in a controlled and systematic approach; this is the driver who omits no detail and leaves nothing to chance, which is essential to ensure that he does not put himself, passengers or any other road user or pedestrian in a potentially dangerous situation at any time or place.

The Driver

As already noted, human error is the cause of many road accidents, and it can be attributed to numerous factors. For example, the driver may have poor powers of concentration, observation, anticipation and patience and may therefore be inclined to be aggressive. He or she may be unable to use the appropriate controls of the vehicle with delicacy and precision as the situation demands. Perhaps because of inadequate knowledge of the workings and mechanics of the vehicle he or she is driving, the driver will have little or no respect for his vehicle — and in return will have poor co-ordination between himself and his vehicle, which can be dangerous at any given time and situation. The driver and vehicle must be in unison at all times.

The Department of Transport conducts over two million 'L' driving tests each year in the United Kingdom. Statistics compiled from that Department show that 53% of candidates fail. This figure proves that driving test candidates are not up to the basic standard of competence to drive; some obviously know this, but still take the test. Additionally, some of the candidates who do pass have done so by sheer luck, because they did not encounter a situation during their test with which they were not competent to cope, should it have arisen. Knowing this, the new so-called 'qualified' driver still takes to the road under the misapprehension that he knows all about driving the type of vehicle on which he took his test. If novice drivers were keen to learn to drive properly, instead of trying to obtain a driving licence as cheaply and as quickly as possible, then another contribution to road safety would be made.

If the people who use our roads each day allowed sufficient time for travel, took more interest in their journey, and concentrated on their driving, instead of using their vehicle as the means of travelling from point 'A' to point 'B' as quickly as possible, then another contribution would be made by the majority to making our overcrowded roads safer to use.

If proof were ever needed that good driving pays a handsome dividend in safety on the road, then a classic example would be that of police officers who have attended and passed the numerous driving courses at Police Driving Schools throughout the United Kingdom, having reached the highest possible standard required of that establishment for the officer to be authorised to drive a particular class of vehicle, or vehicles, in police forces throughout Great Britain. Another significant point is that police drivers keep themselves fit to drive, which assists them to be alert at all times.

A Transport Road Research Laboratory report, No 499 published in December 1972, confirmed that Advanced Motorists have a 50-75% lower accident rate. This indicates the splendid contribution to road safety the 80,000 members of the Institute of Advanced Motorists, and those of ROSPA Advanced Drivers' Association, have made, by proving their driving is well above the average standard. And indeed, the 70,000 members of the Guild of Experienced Motorists have made a major contribution to road safety by driving with care, courtesy and concentration.

The Vehicle

Each year Vauxhall Motors, General Motors and their component manufacturers make a major contribution to road safety by spending millions of pounds on research and development. With the results of the knowledge gained, vehicles and components are being produced with many primary and secondary safety features built into them. Primary safety areas are steering, brakes, chassis and construction, which will assist in avoiding accidents. The secondary safety features are a rigid safety cage for passenger compartment and crumple zones front and rear, which will protect the driver and passengers from injury in the event of an accident. Needless to say, primary features which improve the road-holding capability of the vehicle are not only beneficial to the driver and passengers, but to other road users as well.

We have only to compare vehicles of today with those of a decade or so ago to recognise the improvement in vehicle design and construction, together with the improvements to the interior and the extra equipment supplied with various models, which help to make motoring safer and more enjoyable. Unfortunately there are new vehicles purchased by people who, being aware of the additional safety features incorporated within the vehicles, are at times inclined to abuse the vehicle or be over-confident in the way they drive. Not having the experience to handle a vehicle in the manner in which it is being driven, disaster for the driver or an innocent party frequently results. Some drivers are under the misapprehension that, for example, the tyres fitted to their vehicle will get them out of trouble if the need should arise, regardless of the condition of the road surface or the road speed of the vehicle at the time. The bottom line is that vehicles, however inexpensive or expensive they may be, are only as safe as the people who drive them.

There are some road users whose consideration for or responsibility towards other road users leaves something to be desired. Some people purchase a particular vehicle to promote a self-image, or personalise their existing vehicle with a special colour or colour scheme. The 'bolt-on-goody' brigade and image-seekers who fix superfluous bits and pieces to their vehicles, often drive the vehicle in a manner that can only be described as dangerous. In their opinion they see nothing wrong with their driving, which makes the situation even more serious.

Numerous Governments have updated and introduced new legislation for the road user, in the interest of road safety. Some members of the public disagree with many of the new laws, but if complied with at all times they will give benefit to everybody. Furthermore, roads are being constructed using new technology and materials so that the surface will assist tyres to obtain better adhesion in most weather conditions; this is complemented by improved 'street furniture', which is being placed so that it does not obscure a driver's view, particularly at junctions. A good example is improved replacement lamp posts which make our roads safer to use in all type of weathers, at any time of day or night.

Road Safety

Road Safety is based on the three 'Es' of Education, Engineering and Enforcement.

EDUCATION
These three students who attend a Student Holiday Course at the Harrow Driving Centre, Harrow, Middlesex, are under group instruction.

Right:
ENGINEERING
This underpass in the industrial area at Stevenage, Hertfordshire, has assisted the traffic flow and reduced the risk of accidents.

Education

Teaching of road safety should begin when a child starts to walk, by being guided by the parents, holding its hand or using reins. Once at first and middle schools the child should gain knowledge in general road safety studies.

In the London Boroughs and in the shires in this country, road safety is implemented by Road Safety Officers with the assistance of the teaching staff. The learning of the Green Cross Code throughout the young life of the child is of paramount importance, while the first principles of Roadcraft are taught when cycle and moped training is taken. The experience and knowledge gained from training will assist when the time arrives to learn to drive a motor car.

After passing the Department of Transport driving test, the newly qualified driver who continues to practise what has been learned in the past, assisted by professional instruction, will in time be eligible to take the Advanced Driving Test. For more general instruction, you should contact your local Road Safety Officer (at the town hall or civic centre in the area where you live), who may be able to put you in touch with organisers of 'Better Driving' evening classes or a 'Local Members' group.

It has been the norm for many years for a novice driver to be taught to drive on a one-to-one ratio. The trend today by many training establishments is to give group instruction, whereby one student is behind the wheel and those in the rear of the vehicle will be drawn into the instruction, thus gaining maximal learning.

Engineering

Throughout the history of Britain, people have had to travel from one place to another, for whatever reason. As the quality of roads has improved so has the form of transport. Today, with our numerous motorways, the freedom and ease of travel from one part of the country to another is taken for granted, and at times abused, by the majority of qualified motorcyclists and drivers. Some arrive safely at their destination: some do not. During recent years, road engineering has improved in many ways, from new types of road surface to the design and construction of road junctions, bigger and therefore clearer traffic signs, and more distinguishable road markings. All of these are intended to make the road user's journey easier and as safe as reasonably possible. For example, at crossroads, where road users are entering the junction from different directions, there is potential danger at all times. To alleviate the risk of accidents and to assist traffic flow, roundabouts, flyovers or underpasses have been constructed where two primary routes cross, or where a type of junction has a high-density traffic flow converging.

Regardless of the cost and effort which the authorities have put into the area of need to improve our roads, unless road users change their attitude to the way they drive or ride, all the engineering progress that has been made will be in vain. Inevitably, fatal accidents will occur for one reason or another, considering the volume of traffic on the roads. With the equally inevitable increase in traffic, if a remedial factor is not implemented, accidents too will increase dramatically. The *Highway Code*, if complied with at all times, will assist in the prevention of accidents.

Below left:
A new road surface is being laid with a material which will assist tyres to obtain better adhesion.

Below:
The new lamp posts have been placed further from the edge of the road compared with the old posts; their position, together with the improved lighting they give, provide a contribution to safer motoring.

1. Advanced Driving

Enforcement

Striving for the prevention of road accidents are the police motor patrols and accident prevention units. The continued supervision and observation of the behaviour of all classes of road user — including pedestrians — is aimed at improving the standard of driving by giving advice and assistance as and when needed. When all means of persuasion have failed, enforcement by the legal process is employed to uphold the traffic law.

Speed in itself is not dangerous, but if used at the wrong time or in the wrong place it is lethal. It is therefore the biggest cause of serious road accidents. For this reason we have highly specialised Traffic Patrol Officers, assisted in their duties in accident prevention by sophisticated aids fitted or carried in their vehicles.

In 1983 a total of 718 children, women and men were killed on roads in the Greater London area, compared with 142 deaths caused by criminals. The recent experience of traffic officers

Right:
This speed check sign has been placed by the Accident Prevention Unit of the police to deter road users driving at excessive speeds: some take note of the sign and some do not.

Far right:
**ENFORCEMENT
This police officer is using a Muni Quip T3 model hand-held speed detector which can accurately measure speeds up to 199mph.**

shows that an increasing number of accidents are caused by excessive speed, particularly in built-up areas — vehicles involved tend to be more severely damaged, and it often takes half an hour or more to free people trapped in a car.

To give some idea of when new equipment and traffic management measures were introduced, the following are just some examples of interest. In May 1957, police in London were given powers to remove obstructive and dangerously parked vehicles from the streets. In July of 1958 the parking meter system and radar meters were introduced; and cameras were fitted behind the windscreen of two traffic patrol cars; the idea being to take photographs of dangerous and careless driving incidents as they happened. Thirty-nine traffic wardens started duty in Westminster, London, in September 1960, and in 1964, box markings at road junctions and the 'Give Way' rule at roundabouts were introduced. Today we have many more aids in constant use, assisting the police to enforce the law.

The Cost of a Road Accident

The Department of Transport's *Highways Economic Note No 1, The Cost of Road Accidents 1982*, provided estimates of the cost of road casualties and road accidents of various types.

The Law Concerning Accidents

Should an accident occur on the road and involve personal injury to another person, vehicle or property, the driver must comply with the law:

Accidents

If in any case, owing to the presence of a motor vehicle on the road, an accident occurs whereby personal injury is caused to a person other than the driver of that motor vehicle, or damage is caused to a vehicle other than that motor vehicle, or a trailer drawn thereby, or to an animal other than an animal in or on that motor vehicle or a trailer drawn thereby, the driver of the motor vehicle shall stop and, if required so to do by any person having reasonable grounds for so requiring, give his name and address, and also the name and address of the owner and the identification marks of the vehicle. If for any reason he does not so give his name and address to any such person, such driver shall report the accident at a police station or to a police constable as soon as reasonably practicable and in any case within 24 hours of the accident. Failure to comply with this is an offence.

Driver to produce insurance certificate or report 'injury' accidents

If in any case where owing to the presence on a road of a motor vehicle (other than an invalid carriage), an accident occurs involving personal injury to another person, and the driver of the vehicle does not at the time produce a certificate of insurance or security to a police constable or some person who,

having reasonable grounds for so doing, has required its production, the driver shall, as soon as possible, and in any case within 24 hours, report the accident at a police station or to a police constable and produce his 'certificate'. Failure to do so is an offence; however, he shall not be convicted by reason only of a failure to produce his 'certificate' if within five days after the accident he produces it in person at a police station specified by him at the time the accident was reported. The owner of a motor vehicle is bound to give such information as may be required by, or on behalf of, a chief officer of police, to give for the purpose of determining whether the use of the vehicle was, or was not, properly insured on any occasion when the driver was bound, under this section, to produce his certificate. Failure to do so is an offence. 'Owner' in relation to a vehicle which is the subject of a hiring agreement includes each party to the agreement.

The definition of an accident is 'an unexpected happening, having an adverse physical effect', as stated by Lord Chief Justice Parker. We can endeavour to cost a road accident but never put a true price on it, as each accident varies in severity and quality. We can cost some of the material things which are damaged, or damaged beyond repair in an accident. The cost of a human life or the pain, suffering and grief which some casualties bear at and after a road accident, can never be accurately priced, only estimated.

1982 Average Cost per Casualty (all classes of road user) By Severity

Fatality	£141,300
Serious casualty	£5,970
Slight casualty	£140
Average, all casualties	£4,150

1982 Average Cost per Casualty by Class of Road User

Pedestrians	£6,056
Pedal cyclist	£2.788
Bus and coach occupants	£1,150
Goods vehicle occupants	£4,277
Car and taxi occupants	£3,665
All motorised two-wheeler riders and passengers	£4,028
All motor vehicle users	£3,670
Average, all road users	£4,150

COSTS TO SOCIETY ARISING FROM ROAD ACCIDENTS AND CASUALTIES

The expected cost, to society, of a fatal, serious or slight casualty is the sum of the costs of a number of elements, averaged for each severity of casualty. The information given is regarded as minimum estimates of costs.

- Loss of output due to death or injury. This is calculated as the present value of the expected loss of earnings plus any non-wage payments (national insurance contributions, etc) paid by the employer.
- Ambulance costs and the costs of hospital treatment, etc.
- The costs of pain, grief and suffering to the casualty, relatives and friends. Although they are generally considered to be important, the evaluation of these costs presents difficulties: consequently a notional sum has been included in the estimated costs of fatal, serious and slight casualties.

It is to be noted that the cost of an injury accident is greater than the cost of the corresponding casualty (ie the cost of a fatal accident is greater than the cost of a fatality) for two reasons. The first is that an injury accident is classified according to the most severe casualty, but will on average involve more than one casualty — for example in 1981 a fatal accident on average involved approximately 1.1 fatalities, 0.5 serious casualties and 0.4 slight casualties. The second reason is that there are some costs which are part of the cost of an injury accident which are not specific to casualties. These are:

- Costs of damage to vehicles and property.
- Costs of police and administration of accident insurance.

Injury accident costs vary by class of road because the average number of casualties per injury accident differs from one road class to another. In addition, the cost of vehicle damage per accident varies by class of road. For example, a serious accident on a rural road will on average involve more casualties, and more seriously injured casualties, than on an urban road, together with a greater amount of vehicle damage. Current practice is to calculate average accident costs separately for urban roads, rural roads and motorways.

It may be assumed that on average there will be 6.4 damage-only accidents for every injury accident in urban areas, 4.6 in rural areas and 4.5 on motorways. If injury accidents cannot be differentiated by severity, then as an alternative to making separate calculations for the cost of injury accidents and the cost of damage-only accidents, a total accident cost figure can be calculated by valuing all injury accidents at the Average Accident cost per Injury Accident. This value includes an appropriate allowance for damage-only accidents.

TOTAL ROAD ACCIDENT COSTS IN GREAT BRITAIN IN 1982
In 1982 there were reported 5,447 fatal accidents, 66,139 serious accidents and 184,392 slight accidents. The cost of these 255,978 injury accidents is estimated to have been £1,630 million at 1982 prices and values. In addition there were estimated 1,530,000 damage-only accidents costing a further £745 millions. Total accident costs in 1982 were therefore estimated to have been £2,375 millions. This figure relates to the total cost of accidents to the community, although the incidence of these costs will, of course, vary between groups of road users, and also between road users and other members of society, ie some costs, such as lost output, will not be borne exclusively by casualties themselves, since the taxation and social security systems will ensure that the burden of lost output will be shared by the population at large.

Left:
DRINKING AND DRIVING
To deter the motoring public from drinking and driving, the Breathalyser was introduced in May 1967. In the first year of its use, 9,460 motorists in England and Wales were found guilty by the courts. In 1982, over 75,000 motorists in England and Wales were found guilty as charged, for driving a motor vehicle while under the influence of drink.
The number of convictions for Drinking and Driving is rising each year.

DO NOT DRINK AND DRIVE.

Note that because not all elements of accident costs are quantified, all values should be regarded as minimum values. The variation in cost between classes of road user is because of the different proportions of fatal, serious and slight injuries suffered by casualties from each class of road user.

As mentioned previously, if all road users — including pedestrians — were to concentrate, anticipate and be more patient, the accident rate would be reduced. The money cost of accidents could be saved and put to uses which would benefit the community.

Professional training is essential in any occupation, if a high standard of competence is to be reached and continual use of the knowledge gained assists in achieving the best results at all times. By the end of 1933 the Metropolitan Police had 585 motor vehicles in use. As their fleet of vehicles increased, so did the accident rate, to one accident per 8,000 miles, due to the inadequate standard of driver training and training facilities. For this reason the Metropolitan Police Driving School at Hendon was founded on 7 January 1935. Over the years the School has achieved its objective; to find out how it made such a contribution to road safety, let us have a quick look at the history of Metropolitan Police Transport & Driver Training, as there is much one can learn from it.

1. Advanced Driving

2 50 Years of Metropolitan Police Driver Training

'Hendon trained' is an expression coined many years ago by the popular Press to describe a new standard in driving which is today still a source of pride to the thousands who have passed through the Metropolitan Police Driving School at Hendon. These students have come not only from the Metropolitan and provincial police forces, but also from countries all over the world; for such is the reputation of the School that governments of the dependencies and the Commonwealth have sent men to Hendon so that they might learn at first hand the highly skilled art of driving a motor vehicle safely in all conditions. The events which gave rise to the formation of the Driving School are founded in the more leisurely past, when the gas-lit streets of Victorian London echoed to the clip-clop of horses' hooves as the 'growlers' and the broughams made their sedate way through the West End. The motor car was then a dream, and the sole means of motive power, the horse.

It was in 1758 that law enforcement officers, realising the need for mobility, purchased two horses for the police office at Bow Street. Horses have played an essential part in mobility ever since; in Central London during the middle of the last century, each major police station had its stables from which mounted officers went out daily to patrol their beats. In the then rural extremities of the Metropolitan Police District mounted officers operated from Horse Patrol Stations, patrolling the main coaching roads in much the same way as their present-day colleagues who operate from District Garages.

Probably the first police vehicle was the horse-drawn prison van, a reference to which is made in Police Orders of 1858. These were the Black Marias, so named after Maria Lee, a giant Boston negress whose size and strength was such that when the constables required assistance it was a common thing to send for Maria, who quickly dealt with the trouble makers and marched them off to the lock-up. Today, although the term is extended to all police vans, surprisingly few people are aware of its transatlantic origin.

The Motor Car Act of 1903 was the first statute which applied specifically to the internal combustion engine. Before this, motor cars were governed by legislation which was intended for steam propelled vehicles. Those motor cars which were in being prior to 1898 were subject to the provisions of the Locomotives Act of 1865, which regulated the 'use of locomotives on turnpike and local roads'. This, in effect, meant that every motor car had to be preceded by a man on foot waving a red flag. With the passing of the 1903 Act the motor car, rather belatedly, received its emancipation.

It was in this year that two 7½hp Wolseley touring cars were purchased, for use by the Commissioner and the Receiver, who then, as now, was responsible for administering the finances of the Force. The registration marks allotted to these vehicles, A 209 and A 210, are still associated with the police. A 209 has been retained by the Receiver for his official car, and A 210 for use by the Home Secretary, the Minister answerable to Parliament as the responsible authority for the Metropolitan Police.

As the motor car became the established successor to the horse as a means of transport, so the scope of its commercial use increased, and it was not long before the London criminals realised its potential. Thus was born the 'smash and grab' raid. By 1920 these raids had reached such serious proportions that the Commissioner of the day introduced a new and revolutionary method of policing. The main reason for the success achieved by criminals in this new type of crime was the fact that the police were greatly handicapped by the lack of transport. Not only could the criminal choose the time and place for the raid, but by using a motor vehicle he was almost assured of a complete getaway. In an endeavour to combat this new threat to law and order, four Crossley tenders were made available for the formation of a special squad. Volunteers were called for from PCs in Divisions with driving experience, and after a driving test these officers (together with specially selected detectives) were formed into teams as mobile crime patrols. Working in plain clothes, from the seemingly innocent

Left:
**The 'Black Maria',
1858-1922.**

tenders, the mobile squads achieved an outstanding degree of success, not only against the 'smash and grab' raiders but also against the gangsters, robbers, pick-pockets and petty thieves who were endeavouring to make an easy living in the metropolis. This new and highly successful innovation caught the imagination of the London Press, who referred to the teams as 'flying squads', a name that eventually became the official title for the group of police officers whose almost legendary exploits have made them both feared and respected by the underworld of London. Today the Flying Squad is equipped with

a variety of fast — and not easily identifiable — cars, including Jaguars and Rovers; the drivers attached to the Squad, all of whom have emerged from the Advance Course at the Driving School as Class I drivers, are indeed masters of their art.

The year 1930 is a landmark in the history of police transport. It was in that year that mobile police, now known as Traffic Patrols, came into being as the result of the introduction of the Road Traffic Act of 1930. In their comparatively short history the Traffic Patrols have established a reputation that is second to none, and today competition for selection to the Patrols is as keen as it ever was. Experts in traffic law, vehicle maintenance and road safety, Traffic Patrol men are a powerful arm of the service, destined to play an increasingly important part in the future dominated by the motor vehicle.

Prior to 1932, police drivers were selected from members of the Force with driving experience who possessed sufficient technical knowledge to carry out minor repairs. There was no system of grading according to ability. By 1932, however, due to the expansion of the transport fleet and the increasing variety of vehicles in use, a system of grading was introduced. Although undoubtedly a step in the right direction, it made no provision for instruction or progressive training, but it was at least a sign of the growing awareness within the Force that ultimately it would be necessary to provide some form of training for the drivers of this fast-growing fleet of vehicles.

1932 provided yet another step forward in the history of police transport, for it was in this year that the 'Box System' was introduced. Briefly, this system consisted of the erection of the familiar blue telephone box (immortalised by *Dr Who*) or post on or near every beat as a means of direct communication with the local Sub-Divisional station, by both the patrolling constable and members of the public.

By the end of 1933 the number of vehicles in use by the Force had risen to 585. Unfortunately, as the fleet grew in size, so the number of accidents in which police were involved grew correspondingly, and in the first few months of 1934 the accident mileage ratio rose to one accident for every 8,000 miles. This high rate resulted in considerable adverse comment both in the Press and motoring journals, and as a result of this criticism the Commissioner, Lord Trenchard, arranged for the famous racing motorist Sir Malcolm Campbell to test a number of drivers from Divisions. This difficult and strenuous test consisted of driving a Squad or 'Q' car on normal patrol and on an emergency (999) call, both in heavy traffic and on the open road. Despite the severity of the test and the high standard demanded, all the police drivers passed with flying colours and such was Sir Malcolm Campbell's praise that the ill-founded criticism was silenced. It could not, however, be denied that lack of experience and inadequate training facilities in particular were a great handicap in raising the standard of driving. For these reasons in 1934 the setting up of the Metropolitan Police Driving School at Hendon was ordered.

The introduction of the Driving School caused very little comment, either locally or nationally. Few could have foreseen the impact which the teaching of the School would have on driving technique, not only in this country, but in other lands throughout the world. Nevertheless, 'tall oaks from little acorns

Right:
In 1932 the 'Box System' was introduced; the blue telephone box has now been immortalised by *Dr Who*.

grow', and this is especially true of the Driving School, for the seed so firmly planted in 1934 has today grown into a strong tree, the branches of which stretch far and wide.

So outstanding were the results achieved from the training given to the students who attended the initial Courses that the pattern of future instruction was clear. In 1936 an advance course of driving for Flying Squad, 'Q' car and Traffic Patrol car drivers was introduced, and early in 1937 the Commissioner appointed as his civilian adviser for the training of police drivers one of the most famous racing drivers of the day, the late Earl of Cottenham. Lord Cottenham, who in earlier years had been a member of both the Alvis and Sunbeam racing teams, approached his task with rare zest. His aim was simple — to bring to the technique of advanced driving a new standard of perfection. To this end he personally trained six specially selected Instructors to give this training. In this way the Advanced Car Wing was born, and Lord Cottenham's teaching laid down those many years ago still forms the whole basis of instruction for police drivers. Briefly, his system was that by implementing a simple 'drill' or sequence of events, a driver would ensure that his vehicle was always in the right place at the right time, travelling at the right speed and in the correct gear. Thus, it was reasoned, a driver would be in complete control of any situation with which he might be faced. The success of Lord Cottenham's teaching can best be judged by results, for whilst in 1934 the police vehicle accident rate was one accident in every 8,000 miles, by 1938 it had dropped to one accident in every 27,000 miles. Lord Cottenham's stay with the Metropolitan Police was brief, as he left in 1938, but the impact of his teaching remains, and the system of driving which he initiated has resulted in a police vehicle mileage for each blameworthy accident in 1982 of 26,108 for cars, 86,842 for motor cycles; proof if proof was ever needed, that good driving and training pays a handsome dividend in safety on the road.

The use of motor cycles in the Force has increased rapidly since the Chater-Lea combination made its brief appearance in 1924. They were found to be invaluable (as indeed they are today) for getting to the forefront of traffic jams, and their increased use, mainly by Traffic Patrols, has grown with the passing years, not only as an aid in keeping London's traffic moving, but for escorting large and cumbersome loads, providing escorts for visiting Royalty and Heads of State, and enforcing the provisions of the Road Traffic Acts.

Although the Motor Cycle Wing of the Driving School was introduced in 1938, the training of motor cyclists had in fact commenced much earlier. In January 1936 a few selected Traffic Patrol officers were tested as to their suitability to ride motor cycles, and these tests subsequently developed into two-day courses. These short courses soon exposed the need for fuller training, and so the Motor Cycle Wing was added to the Standard and Advanced Car Wings as an integral part of the School.

One of the first postwar tasks undertaken by the Driving School was the training of a number of Ministry of Transport driving examiners. These examiners were given a special two-week course with the Advanced Wing, so that in carrying out their important task of testing members of the public, they would at least themselves have the best possible yardstick with which to measure the standard of others. Unfortunately the task of training all the Ministry examiners was too big for the School to undertake in addition to its normal commitments, and eventually the Ministry of Transport had, of necessity, to institute its own training programme.

Since their introduction in 1930, the work of the Traffic Patrols had increased rapidly with each succeeding year. As more and more vehicles poured on to already inadequate roads, and new types with a variety of technical improvements left the factories annually, traffic legislation rapidly reached a state where some form of specialist study was needed to enable the Traffic Patrols to carry out their work efficiently. In order to provide training in this specialised field, the Traffic Patrol Wing was introduced in 1948. Its initial task was to give preliminary instruction to officers selected for Traffic Patrol duty. Later, in 1959, an advanced level course was organised for the older, more experienced officers to fit them for operating the specially equipped traffic accident cars. Both courses are still in being. They are constantly being revised to keep pace with the ever increasing complexity of the traffic problem in the metropolis, and the comprehensive instruction given to students attending the Traffic Patrol Wing provides a firm foundation for the many and varied daily duties which the Traffic Patrols are required to carry out.

During the Earl of Cottenham's term of office at the School, the method of teaching on both Car Wings was standardised, so that all students had the same curriculum. Each instructor possessed his own set of duplicated notes, and the students were required to copy out pages and pages of notes covering each phase of instruction — a laborious process. In 1955, however, it was decided that the teaching of the School might well benefit the general motoring public, and so the sheaf of typewritten notes used so effectively by countless instructors was edited, and printed by Her Majesty's Stationery Office. It appeared as *Roadcraft*. Almost overnight it became a best seller, and to date well over a quarter of a million copies have been sold. *Roadcraft*, and its sister publication, the *Highway Code*, are the books which form the basis of every police driver's training, and the motorist who reads, understands and acts upon the advice and instruction given therein is well on the way to becoming a very good driver.

On completing the Standard Car Course, students were returned to Divisions to gain practical experience, and after completing some 15,000 to 20,000 miles they were eligible to be tested as to their suitability for an Advanced Course. In very many cases the sudden transition from the low-powered general purpose cars and vans on which the driver had gained his experience to the high-powered cars of the Advanced Wing was too much, and so in 1957 the Intermediate Course was introduced. Of two weeks duration, this course provided a 'half way' stage at which students received instruction in driving medium-powered cars. Drivers who successfully completed this Intermediate Course were returned to Divisions to gain further experience prior to an Advanced Course. They were then entitled to drive radio-equipped patrol cars, and the experience thus gained soon paid a handsome dividend in an ever higher standard of driving when students attended the Advanced Course.

We have seen that the growth of the transport fleet, new methods of policing and the constant need to train police drivers to even higher standards of skills and efficiency, has increased the work of the Driving School. From those two Wolseley cars in 1903, the fleet has grown to number nearly 3,700 vehicles of all types, and the primary but no means the only function of the Driving School is to ensure that the officers who volunteer and are selected for driving duties are trained to the highest possible standard.

At the present time there are over 17,000 authorised drivers, and the annual mileage driven by them on police duty exceeds 41 million miles. In a fleet which comprises a multiplicity of makes and types of vehicle, from the 50cc moped for traffic wardens up to the 42-seat coach and heavy goods vehicles, training must be both wide and comprehensive to include riot situation control and anti-hijack techniques. Instruction must be of the highest calibre to get the best out of each student, and the organisation of the School must be kept at a constant peak of efficiency, at the same time being flexible enough to meet changing circumstances, often at short notice.

The School is under the direct control of the Commandant and his deputy and is part of the 'D' Department Training Scheme. It is divided into wings, each under the supervision of an Inspector who is in turn responsible to a Chief Inspector. The instructional staff consists of about 36 sergeants, 39 constables, and one senior and 29 civilian driving instructors. There is also attached to the School a small clerical support staff, a store keeper and a model maker.

The Standard Car Wing runs Novice Training, Standard District, Traffic Patrol Standard Driving and Van Driver courses, and the Advanced Car and Driving Instructor courses. Also provided are Heavy Goods Vehicle, Motor Cycle Wing and Technical Training Wing courses.

Advanced Car Course

This course is of six weeks duration and is divided into two parts known as Phase I and Phase II.

Phase I

This is of two weeks duration and the students selected are experienced Standard or Van drivers, who are expected to study *Roadcraft*, *Highway Code* and Transport Regulations prior to attending the Driving School to refresh their previous learning. The course starts with a written examination and practical reversing examination and the following two weeks is used to ensure the student can drive to the System or Car Control up to the national speed limit and control the car on the skid pan at a higher speed than that allowed on the Standard Course. At the end of the Phase I course, he is examined on an assessment drive to test whether he is suitable to progress to Phase II.

Phase II

This course is of four weeks duration and the entire course is spent driving, with familiarisation of coaches, articulated vehicles and Land Rovers/Range Rovers, with both on-road driving and off-road driving over rough country. The course is designed to ensure that only the very best pass the final driving test, which is the climax of the whole six weeks' rigorous practical driving experience. Although the foundation of this advanced course was started at standard driving level, skidding instruction, bandit pursuit training and high speed driving form a major part of the Advanced Course. Alternating from day to day through a mixed fleet of vehicles, both manual and automatic gear boxed, including the Rover 2600 and 3500, Carlton, Cortina and Granada 2.8, students quickly learn to handle a wide variety of vehicles with skill and confidence. Building up progressively to speeds that are within 10mph of the vehicle's maximum speed, they rapidly acquire the expert knowledge needed to drive fast but with perfect safety. The training on the skid pan is an aid to their safety training.

Contrary to popular belief, skidding instruction at the School is not given for the purpose of teaching students to skid. Quite the opposite in fact, for the main object of the instruction is to teach how to get the maximum out of the car in varying road and climatic conditions without skidding and it is only secondary to teach how to correct a skid. One has only to see the skid-pan instructors 'drifting' a car round and round the skid-pan, without allowing it to break away, to realise the importance of this instruction.

The final drive on the Advanced Course is in three parts. After a preliminary 'warm up' to get the feel of the car which has an automatic gearbox, the student is told by the examiner that he has received an imaginary '999' call which he is to answer. At this the student is required to get the best out of the car under the traffic conditions, but at the same time to obey scrupulously all speed limits and road signs. At the same time he has to give a running commentary on what he can see, what he cannot see but must consider, say what he is doing and why he is doing it. This is no easy matter, particularly at high speed, but unless the student has developed the ability to plan well ahead, he will be forced into errors of his own making. After he has travelled about eight miles the student will be told to resume normal patrol. They will then stop at a pre-arranged location, where the student and examiner will change to a manual gearbox car and after a warm up period in the different vehicle the student is told to watch out for a particular stolen car. Needless to say it is not

METROPOLITAN POLICE DRIVING SCHOOL, HENDON

Below:
Students receiving instruction in car control on the School skid-pan.

2. 50 Years of Metropolitan Police Driver Training

very long before this car appears, driven by an Advanced Wing instructor who proceeds to do everything possible to lose the student. The student's task is to keep within striking distance of the 'bandit', but not to overtake or try to stop him or put himself or members of the public in danger, and at the same time give a running commentary of his own actions and that of the bandit. After a further 12 miles, the chase is called off and the test is over.

At the end of the drive the student is assessed. If he gains 86% or over, he is graded a Class I driver, if he gains between 75% and 85% he is graded Class II, if he is assessed below 75% he remains a van driver. The successful students have received over nine weeks of intensive training (11 weeks if novices) and are fitted to take their place with those who are regarded as the finest drivers in the country.

Technical Training Wing

Traffic Patrols play a particularly important part in the constant police endeavour to educate road users and stem the rising tide of traffic accident casualties. Thoughtless parking, negligent driving, defective vehicles and the disregard of road signs, are all contributory causes to accidents; the specialist training given to Traffic Patrol officers on the Technical Training Wing is designed to instruct them not only in the prevention of accidents, but to thoroughly investigate the cause when they occur, and at the same time teach them how best to keep London's traffic moving. To fit them for these duties, a sound knowledge of traffic law, vehicle construction, accident investigation and tachograph calibration is necessary. This tuition is given at Standard and Advanced level, with specialist courses such as Fatal Accident Vehicle Examiners' courses arranged as required. Lectures on traffic law cover such diverse subjects as the various Road Traffic Acts, Motor Vehicle Construction & Use Regulations, Registration, Licensing, Lighting, Driving Licences, Insurance, Goods Vehicles, Drivers' Hours, Tachographs, Cabs, PSVs, Road Works, Pedestrian Crossings, Traffic Signs and Transportation of Hazardous Substances to name but a few. Considerable time is also devoted to studying the construction of component parts such as brakes, steering, tyres, etc, and the defects which wear or lack of maintenance cause in these parts.

Driving Instructor Course

This is one of the most important courses at the Driving School. If the wrong personnel are finally selected to join the instructional staff, the whole concept of prestige in the term 'Hendon trained' could be undermined.

The course is of six weeks duration and police students themselves should be Advanced Drivers, having attended Hendon for their previous instruction. It consists of intensive training in both driving and classroom instructional techniques. Written/practical examinations on *Roadcraft*, *Highway Code*, Mechanics, Transport Regulations require a pass mark of 85% in all subjects to qualify. The course is then followed by a period of practical teaching of students under supervision on Standard Courses, before being finally accepted with the ultimate goal of progressing to an Advanced Course Instructor.

Courses for Civilian Instructors are run on the same lines, but their instruction does not progress beyond Standard and Van Driver Training and many of the civilian driving instructors are recruited from previous police instructors/drivers.

The Driving School Today

Over and above the main courses mentioned, refresher, re-classification and special courses are held as necessary; as a result, approximately 4,500 students are trained each year. In addition, the Driving School receives over 500 visitors from all walks of life annually, and instructors are constantly in demand as lecturers at schools, motor and motorcycle clubs and business organisations.

Metropolitan Police teams have also entered the highly competitive field of rallying, and competitions are entered against the Army MT school, in such events as 'Copdrive'. Motorcyclists from the School, Traffic Patrol and Districts compete each year in the Services, Scottish six-day and other such trials with a good deal of success — all of them 'Hendon trained'.

So we have moved from the past to the present, from the horse-drawn Black Marias of 1858 to the power-packed vehicles of today. During the past 50 years the Metropolitan Police Driving School has occupied its place as a world leader in driver training and its methods have been adopted and copied throughout the world. Graduates from the School are scattered in their thousands, not only in Metropolitan London but all over the civilised world. To all of them 'Hendon' means something more than a dot on the map. It evokes, in each and every one of them, a blend of nostalgia and inner pride, for wherever motorists gather or motoring is discussed the expression 'Hendon trained' still stands for all that is best in driving.

The School motto is *Experientia Docet — Experience Teaches* — and may it ever be passed on.

3 Car Control

It must be appreciated that during the time the Earl of Cottenham was at Hendon, instructors from Chelmsford (Essex) and Hutton (Lancs) were taught the System of Car Control by him, therefore the three original Police Driving Schools in the United Kingdom were, Hendon, Chelmsford and Hutton.

Today there are 42 Police Driving Schools in the United Kingdom, all teaching to the standard of Hendon, although the courses may differ according to their needs.

Accidents

Of the three contributory factors to the cause of a road accident, human error and the presence of a human being is directly

Left:
The first driver to be killed in a motor accident in Great Britain was a Mr E. R. Sewell, driver and head tester for the Daimler Motor Co; a passenger also died. The accident happened at the bottom of Grove Hill, Harrow, Middlesex, in 1899, and was caused by the driver applying the brakes suddenly: the wooden spokes were not strong enough to bear the strain on them and therefore the rear wheels collapsed.

Right:
Looking at the double white lines at their furthest point informs the driver that there is a left-hand bend ahead. Therefore at this point a reduction of speed should be made.

Below right:
The speed of the vehicle was too fast. The foot brake had been applied too late and too hard, and the driver lost control of his vehicle. It continued on a straight course, crossing the white line, colliding with a lamp post and mounting the verge. The vehicle has come to rest in woodland; there was no injury to the driver.

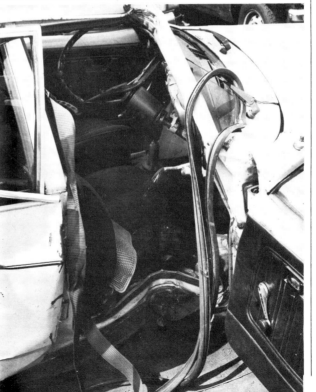

Far left:
Another typical example of excessive speed at the wrong time and place. Note the skid marks: the vehicle has struck the tree.

Left:
Think what the passenger must have looked like.

Below left:
The driver of this vehicle received chest and leg injuries. Note the position of the steering wheel and column.

3. Car Control

The Push and Pull Method of Steering

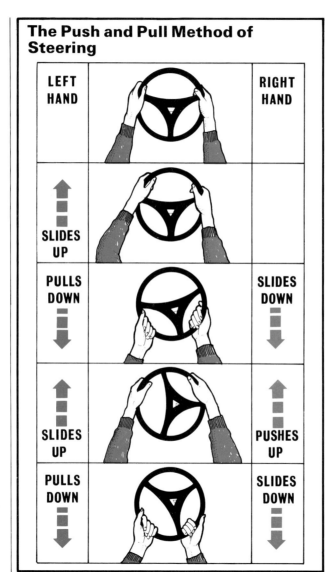

LEFT HAND		RIGHT HAND
SLIDES UP ⬆		
PULLS DOWN ⬇		SLIDES DOWN ⬇
SLIDES UP ⬆		PUSHES UP ⬆
PULLS DOWN ⬇		SLIDES DOWN ⬇

Right:
STEERING
The accompanying diagram illustrates hand and steering movements for turning left. For a turn to the right the first steering movement will be the right hand pulling down from the 12 o'clock position.

responsible for almost every one. The Police System of Car Control as devised many years ago by the Earl of Cottenham is a simple and ordered method of driving in which the driver omits no detail and leaves nothing to chance, thus giving time and distance to react to any situation. If the driver of the car in the accompanying illustrations had been in the right place on the road at the right time, travelling at the right speed and in the correct gear, he would have been in complete control.

Driving Position and Steering

The driver should be in control of the vehicle at all times. One contributory factor to this end is the position in which the driver sits whilst driving. There are some drivers who slouch in the driving seat or sit too close to the steering wheel. There are others who sit too far back, seat partially reclined and with arms fully extended, and have difficulty operating the foot pedals and hand controls properly — often imitating their heroes in the world of motor sport, whom they follow and try to copy, but on the public highway.

The ideal seating position must be found to suit the stature of the individual driver. If practically possible the driving seat should be adjusted so that the pedals can be operated without fuss and discomfort and so that hand controls and auxiliary switches are within easy reach. The driver should sit upright and alert, not taut or strained, yet not too relaxed. The steering characteristics built in as a design feature in one make of car may not be included in another, thus steering may be light in one car and heavy in another. The vehicle may respond more (oversteer) or less (understeer) than the driver expects; the steering movement may be power assisted. The driver must quickly adapt himself to the feel of the vehicle he is driving, so that he is able to place it where he wants it, in all conditions.

Both hands should remain on the wheel unless it is necessary to remove one or other to signal, operate an auxiliary switch or to change gear, etc. Any change from the straight course must be accomplished gradually and smoothly, other than when manoeuvring at slow speeds. The steering wheel should be turned by the 'Pull and Push' method as shown in the accompanying diagram. Most vehicles have steering which is self-straightening and control will be necessary to prevent the steering wheel from spinning back, which is lazy driving and potentially dangerous. Accordingly, the steering wheel should be fed back by hand movements, in the reverse order to which it was originally turned.

Far left:

THE IDEAL DRIVING POSITION
The driver's back should be well supported by the seat and the left leg should be comfortable when the clutch pedal is pressed fully down. The driver's hands should be placed naturally with the palms on the rim of the wheel, fingers should fold around the rim resting lightly but ready to grip when necessary. The hands should be at a 'ten to two' position (as on a clock face), arms slightly bent.

Above left:
Elbows must not be placed on the window frame, arm rests, etc, because this reduces control. On slippery roads, all steering movements should be delicate, otherwise skids may be induced. Hands should be placed on the wheel in the 'ten to two' or 'quarter to three' position: not gripping tightly but ready to exert maximum leverage if necessary. The driver should not cross his hands when turning the wheel, as precise steering control cannot be obtained.

Left:
The sign warns the driver of the possibility of side wind that could blow the vehicle off course. The driver should make himself aware of which direction the wind is blowing.

Side Wind

3. Car Control

Acceleration

Each year, vehicle manufacturers spend vast sums of money designing vehicles for the future. However, the benefits of sleek aerodynamic shapes with low drag factors, which assist the driver to gain high mileage for the minimum of petrol used, are often wasted by the driver employing the accelerator incorrectly. There are some drivers who are unaware of the fact that the performance capabilities of different vehicles vary considerably according to the efficiency of the engine and power-to-weight ratio: they purchase a family saloon car expecting — and demanding — the same performance as a very special high powered sports car — often with fatal results, as statistics prove.

The term 'acceleration' in this context means that when pressure is exerted on the accelerator, the road speed of the motor vehicle will increase. Acceleration affects the behaviour of a vehicle as it travels along the road, more so when moving off from a stationary position. It is either pushed along (rear-wheel drive), pulled along (front-wheel drive) or pulled and pushed at the same time (four-wheel drive). These different types of transmission have their own individual influence on the stability of the vehicle. When hard pressure is suddenly applied on the accelerator, it will induce wheel spin, then skidding (more so on a slippery road surface), and finally cause the vehicle to drive through a curved path; therefore heavy acceleration should be avoided if tyre adhesion with the road is to be maintained. For these reasons it is also desirable that acceleration is applied only when the vehicle is travelling on a straight path, because the vehicle is most stable when the weight is evenly distributed.

A thorough understanding of the accelerator, gears, brakes and steering is essential. With intelligent use of these controls the system of Car Control can be developed. It is surprising that many drivers are unaware that they misuse the accelerator until they receive professional driving instruction to improve their skill. A good driver will use the accelerator precisely at the right time and place, avoiding sudden and coarse movements which result in uneven and thus jerky vehicle control. It should be borne in mind that speed may be reduced by deceleration when the pressure on the pedal is eased: the engine will slow down due to the compression in the cylinders, and thus slowing down will be transmitted to the driving wheels. As engine-induced deceleration is a gradual process, it will have little effect on the adhesion of the tyres on the road. The loss of road speed by engine deceleration will also be more effective when a low gear is engaged. This should be borne in mind when driving on roads that have a slippery surface when normal braking could induce skidding, and to assist braking when descending steep hills. A driver is advised to wear light footwear, preferably shoes, because thick-soled, heavy boots or shoes will restrict the sensation of pedal movement.

Acceleration Sense

The object of Feature Six in the system of Car Control is to consider and apply the correct degree of acceleration required for the turn and exit of the hazard so that it can be completed safely, with due regard for the type of road surface, the actual and potential presence of other vehicles and the speed that it is safe to travel for the conditions prevailing at the time. For these reasons the vehicle should be travelling in the right place on the road, at the right speed, and with the correct gear engaged. In so doing, it will be contributing to the driver's safety in certain potentially dangerous situations. It will also be possible to accelerate out of danger as well as to brake, bearing in mind that in particular situations braking could result in stopping in the path of approaching danger, when acceleration would have enabled the driver to avoid the danger.

Acceleration sense can be applied to every facet of driving. There are many drivers who do not combine observation with acceleration sense, eg maintaining a constant speed when coming up behind a slower vehicle, then find it necessary to brake hard; or, on leaving a hazard, applying acceleration when it is obvious that there is a traffic hold-up ahead. A skilled driver will use the information gained by good powers of observation, and drive with efficiency and with the minimum wear to the vehicle.

Braking

A novice motorcyclist who has a keen interest in life will enrol with a training organisation appointed by the Department of Transport, which will teach him good machine control, plus many more aspects of riding. One facet of riding that should always be borne in mind is the type of road surface and its condition: never ride or drive at a speed that will create danger to oneself or others. The average motorist drives at a speed well outside the bounds of safety for the prevailing conditions, unaware of the state or type of road surface. It is easy to recognise the fault after the event has occurred.

In normal driving conditions, primary braking must be by proper use of the brake and not by using the gears. For all

Left:
CLOSING THE GAP
When the road ahead cannot be seen to be clear the skilled driver, catching up with another vehicle, will have eased off the accelerator in good time, using deceleration as a brake. At the same time he will be in a correct position to overtake when the road ahead can be seen to be clear.

3. Car Control

THINKING DISTANCE at 30mph
Distance travelled during reaction time

Time (sec)	Distance (ft/m)	Time (sec)	Distance (ft/m)
.175	7.7/2.3	.475	20.9/6.3
.2	8.8/2.7	.5	22 /6.7
.225	9.9/3.0	.525	23.1/7.0
.25	11 /3.3	.55	24.2/7.3
.275	12.1/3.7	.575	25.3/7.7
.3	13.2/4.0	.6	26.4/8.0
.325	14.3/4.3	.625	27.5/8.3
.35	15.4/4.7	.65	28.6/8.7
.375	16.5/5.0	.675	29.7/9.0
.4	17.6/5.3	.7	30.8/9.3
.425	18.7/5.7	.725	31.9/9.7
.45	19.8/6.0	.75	33 /10.0

REMEMBER — This does *not* include braking distance which at 30mph is a further 45ft.

TOTAL STOPPING DISTANCE
Distance travelled assuming an about average reaction time

Speed (mph)	Reaction Distance (ft/m)	Braking Distance (ft/m)	Total Stopping Distance (ft/m)
20	20/ 6.0	20/ 6.0	40/12.0
30	30/ 9.1	45/13.6	75/22.7
40	40/12.0	80/24.0	120/36.0
50	50/15.1	125/37.9	175/53.0
60	60/18.2	180/54.6	240/73.0
70	70/21.1	245/74.2	315/95.3

REMEMBER — These braking distances only apply on *dry* road surfaces. On wet roads, they could double.

Above right:
The average driver will take 0.7 seconds to respond to a sudden situation. In that time the distance travelled would be 30.8ft for a vehicle travelling at 30mph.

Right:
From the moment the driver applies the brake to the time the vehicle comes to rest is called the braking or stopping distance.

normal braking the initial free movement of the pedal should be taken up gently, and pressure progressively increased as necessary until it can be relaxed as the unwanted road speed is lost. When braking to a standstill the final effort should be so judged that the vehicle is brought to a gliding halt without jerking or suddenly settling down at the rear end. Secondary braking is braking using the gears.

Apart from other considerations, the speed of a vehicle at any time must not exceed the speed at which it can be stopped within the distance the driver can see to be clear. The driver must know the distance he needs to slow down appreciably or stop, from all road speeds. Not only must he know the distances, but must be able to relate them to the road on which he is travelling. On a good dry road the average vehicle should

be capable of stopping in the distances as shown in the *Highway Code*.

Reaction time may be defined as the time that passes between the moment the driver observes the need for action and the moment he takes that action. The average driver takes 0.7sec from seeing an emergency situation to placing his foot on the brake pedal. The distance covered in that time is known as the 'thinking distance' and will be the same figure in feet as the speed in mph, eg 30mph=30ft. Thinking distance+braking distance=stopping distance.

The thinking distance will vary in four ways:

(a)   With the speed of the vehicle.

(b)   With the physical and mental condition of the driver.

(c)   With the degree of concentration being applied at the time.

(d)   With what can and cannot be seen to be clear at the time.

Controlled, progressive braking is preferable to a sudden hard application of the brake pedal. To maintain stability of the car, and equal distribution of weight while braking, the following rules should be applied:

(1)   Brake firmly only when travelling in a straight line.

(2)   Vary brake pressure according to the condition of the road surface.

(3)   Brake in good time, well before reaching the hazard.

(4)   When descending a steep winding hill, brake firmly on the straight stretches and ease off the brake in the bends. Remember the value of engaging a low gear at an early stage in the descent.

Far left:
The braking distance should be trebled when braking on a slippery surface like cobblestones or wooden blocks. Skidding will occur from the slightest cause in the wet.

Left:
This sign in the Austrian Alps warns the driver to 'Check the Brakes!'. The driver should check the movement of handbrake and footbrake when he first enters the car, and the footbrake again as soon as possible after moving off.

3.   Car Control

Road Surfaces and Tyre Care

The average motorist is not as aware of the different types of road surface he drives on as he should be. It is useless to complain about a slippery road surface after a skid has occurred. The Advanced Driver, who looks well ahead, thus recognising any change in road surface in good time, will appreciate and apply the correct values of braking, acceleration, steering and road speed on the approach to bends and other hazards, so that maximum road-holding is always achieved.

The majority of roads when dry are good or fairly good for road-holding, However, when the weather is wet the road surface becomes slippery: this is especially the case following a long spell of dry weather, when rubber dust and oil get washed to the road surface and cause tyres to lose adhesion. The presence of ice, frost, snow, mud and wet leaves have their own distinctive appearance, and must not be ignored, because they are factors that affect control of the vehicle.

It must be borne in mind that during wintry weather, road surfaces become frosty and ice-covered, and more so on bridges or flyovers because of the cold air flowing beneath them. The experienced driver will be aware of the danger of any area of road that is shaded, because ice could be present, and will take due precautions in good time to avoid skidding. Note that tyres travelling on ice make virtually no noise.

The good driver will look out for deep potholes, projecting manhole covers, sunken gullies and any other objects likely to damage tyres. A deep pothole, if ignored while travelling at speed round a bend, could cause the driver to lose effective steering control (course) and the rear of the vehicle could start tramping round the bend, which could have disastrous consequences. When intending to park the vehicle on the road, the driver should bring the vehicle to rest in a safe place and position, close to the kerb yet avoiding tyre contact with it, thus preventing damage to the tyre(s).

Right:
The lustre on a road surface is a good clue to the presence of ice, and due care must be taken at all times. If a driver should ever drive into a lump of frozen slush like the one shown here, the consequence could be the same as that of driving into a lump of concrete.

Far right:
Mud on the road can have the same effect on tyre adhesion as that of ice.

Far left above:
Reflecting road studs (sometimes referred to as 'cat's-eyes') first came into use in 1934. It has been estimated that seven million studs of various types are being used in Britain. The road surface of asphalt, with a dressing of stones has a comparatively high non-skid value. However, the cat's-eye protrudes from the road surface, which can be a danger to the motorcyclist, particularly when wet.

Above left:
Harsh braking and acceleration should be avoided on wet leaves.

Left:
A slight change of course must be made to avoid deep potholes, projecting manhole covers and other objects to avoid damage to tyres.

3. Car Control

Right:
When intending to park his vehicle on the road, the driver should bring the vehicle to rest close to the kerb, as shown in the picture.

Below right:
The driver of this vehicle has scuffed the tyres on the kerb, which will in all probability damage the walls of the tyre(s). In consequence, a blow-out could occur at any time.

Below:
It is of the utmost importance that tyre pressures and the condition of the tyres are checked regularly. Any defect found should be rectified as soon as practically possible.

Skidding

Skidding is defined as the involuntary movement of the vehicle due to grip of the tyres on the road becoming less than a force or forces acting on the vehicle. In other words a vehicle skids when one or more of the tyres lose normal grip on the road.

Any driver who has experienced a skid will remember that he was changing either the speed or direction of the vehicle immediately prior to the skid developing. It will therefore be realised that skids are usually caused by accelerating, braking or changing direction, these manoeuvres being carried out so suddenly or forcibly that forces are created which are more powerful than the grip of the tyres on the road. It therefore follows that the more slippery the road surface, the less powerful are the forces needed to break the grip of the tyres.

The following are causes of skidding, either singly or in combination:

● Excessive speed for the existing circumstances — this is a basic cause.
● Coarse steering in relation to a speed which is not in itself excessive.
● Harsh acceleration.
● Excessive or sudden braking.

It is therefore essential that each type of skid is recognised in the early stages of development if corrective measures are to be taken.

Rear Wheel Skid

This occurs when the rear wheels lose their grip on the road and the vehicle may swing to either direction. If unchecked, the rear wheel skid can cause the vehicle to turn broadside or completely round. Eliminate the cause by relaxing pressure on the accelerator or brake pedal, and at the same time turn the steering wheel in the direction of the skid, ie if the rear wheels slide to the left, turn the steering wheel to the left. When stability has been regained the vehicle can be steered on to the desired course. Excess or prolonged steering correction should be avoided or another skid may be induced in the opposite direction.

Front Wheel Skid

This occurs usually on a corner or bend when the front wheels lose their grip, and the vehicle does not travel in the direction in which it is being steered. It can be caused by excessive speed, coarse steering or excessive or sudden braking, and in the case

Left:
The driver approached a left hand bend too fast. In so doing the rear of the car has lost adhesion and veered off to the right, causing the driver to apply corrective measures by releasing the accelerator and steering to the right, as can be seen. The driver must be prepared for the possibility of a secondary skid.

3. Car Control

Right:
The driver approached a right hand bend too fast. In so doing the rear of the car has lost adhesion and veered off to the left, causing the driver to apply corrective measures by releasing the accelerator and steering to the left, as can be seen. The driver must be prepared for the possibility of a secondary skid.

of a front wheel drive vehicle, harsh acceleration. Eliminate the cause by relaxing the accelerator or brakes, momentarily straighten the steering to allow the front wheels to regain their grip, and then gently steer on to course. In front wheel drive vehicles the driver should be prepared for the sudden grip of the front wheels as deceleration becomes effective.

Four Wheel Skid

This occurs when all wheels lose their grip on the road. It is usually associated with excessive or sudden braking, and the effects on the vehicle may be a combination of those encountered in a rear or front wheel skid. On slippery surfaces the driver may experience a sensation of an increase rather than a decrease of speed. The next action will normally be dictated by traffic conditions, but usually there is need for a quick reduction in speed. On dry roads this will be achieved by maintaining the pressure on the brake pedal. Where, however, directional control is more important, and in all cases on wet or slippery roads, the cause of the skid must be eliminated by relaxing the pressure on the brake pedal, thus allowing the wheels to revolve again to regain control. It should be remembered that a four wheel skid may also be a progression from a front or rear wheel skid which has not been corrected.

When driving on very slippery roads, smooth control is essential. Any braking, steering or gear changing must be carried out so that tyre adhesion is not broken. When moving off or travelling at low speeds the selection of a higher gear than normal may be advantageous to reduce the possibility of wheel spin.

General

If a skid is allowed to develop fully a driver will rarely find that he has enough space to correct it. Concentration and good observation are essential if skids are to be avoided, and quick reactions are necessary when a skid does occur.

It is important to stress that on very slippery roads, the best control of speed is through the accelerator with a suitable gear engaged. Reduction of the speed on a slippery surface is best done by the selection of a lower gear, but it is essential that the gear change is made as smoothly as possible with accurate matching of engine revolutions to the road speed before the clutch is finally engaged.

Skidding instruction is given for three reasons:

(a) To raise the standard of driving, to give the highest degree of all-round efficiency.
(b) To give confidence in driving under any conditions.
(c) To equip the driver to meet any emergency which might arise.

It must be borne in mind that skidding must *not* be practised on public roads.

Gear Changing

No matter how well a driver may handle a vehicle, his use of the gearbox will do much to make or mar his driving. Therefore it is surprising how many drivers misuse the gears every time they drive. One of the hallmarks of a good driver is the ability to change gear smoothly at the right time and place: having selected the correct gear for the situation, is able to be in proper control of the vehicle, and follow the dictates of roadcraft, economy and safety. The essential ingredients in changing gear correctly are the ability to accurately match engine revolutions to road speed, together with precise operation of clutch, accelerator and gears.

Faults

- Moving off from stationary in second gear, creating excessive engine speed and unnecessary wear to the clutch. First gear should be used to get the vehicle over the initial stage of inertia, then a higher gear selected as appropriate. On a down start it is acceptable to start in second gear providing no undue wear occurs.
- Braking and changing gear at the same time, which is a control fault. All unwanted road speed should be lost by proper use of the footbrake, then the required gear selected. A gear change should not be made in the initial stages of braking. The 'Heel and Toe method' (heel on the brake and toe on the accelerator) when braking and changing gear at the same time is not good driving and can be dangerous. Therefore it should not be used.
- Changing to a lower gear to slow down, instead of using the brakes, with the exception of brake failure or on a slippery road.
- Changing to a lower gear on a 'closing gap', followed by another gear change and a hurried application of the brakes. The correct method is proper use of brakes until all unwanted speed has been lost, then select the appropriate gear to match that of the road speed of the vehicle.
- Poor co-ordination between hand and foot to make a clean smooth gear change.
- Changing gear at the wrong time and place, ie, while overtaking, on a corner or bend. The gear should be selected on the approach to the hazard, not in it.
- When moving off, going through all the gears as quickly as possible, then having to change down again due to unmatched gear and road speed, when it was obvious that

Left:
GEAR SELECTION
On a steep down gradient a low gear should be engaged to assist control speed with engine compression, thereby avoiding long periods of sustained braking.

Below:
On a slippery road such as this it would be safer to use the engine compression to lose speed rather than braking, since the latter would be liable to cause skidding.

3. Car Control

an intermediate gear was suitable for the prevailing conditions.

- Going through the gearbox gear by gear, when intermediate gears can be by-passed, eg 4-2 or 2-4.
- Not being aware of the correct degree of acceleration needed to accelerate safely out of a hazard (Feature Six in the System of Car Control) due to the incorrect gear being engaged at the time. This could put the driver in a potentially dangerous situation.

It is of paramount importance that the driver is aware of the minimum and maximum speed of each gear of the vehicle he is driving, because the correct use of gears is part of car sympathy. A driver who concentrates and respects the vehicle being driven will in time change gear with delicacy and smoothness, and thus be on the way to acquiring a polished driving style, the ultimate aim of the Advanced Driver.

Gear Selection Faults with Automatic Transmission

- Failure to apply the handbrake or footbrake before engaging 'D' or 'R' from stationary. This is potentially dangerous if the choke is in use.
- Starting (if the vehicle permits) the engine in 'P' rather than 'N', which would avoid going through reverse, with a cold or high revving engine.
- Selecting a lower gear 'L' at too high a road speed.
- Moving the selector to 'N' when making temporary stops.
- Not applying the handbrake when the vehicle has stopped with a gear engaged and the footbrake not in use.

The Handbrake

Under normal conditions the handbrake should not be applied until the vehicle is stationary. The pawl release should be operated when the handbrake is applied, to prevent wear to the ratchet. As experience is gained, it will not be necessary to apply the handbrake for every momentary stop. However, when the vehicle has been stopped and the intention of the driver is to leave the vehicle, the handbrake should be applied. This rule is a legal requirement and must be adhered to strictly; otherwise a dangerous situation could occur.

When driving a vehicle fitted with automatic transmission the driver should be aware that the vehicle may 'creep' when stationary with the engine ticking over and the gear selector lever in 'D' or 'R' (or equivalent position). To prevent the vehicle moving unexpectedly, the handbrake should be applied. If circumstances mean the vehicle is likely to be stationary for longer than a normal hold-up, Neutral should be selected. When starting a cold engine that has a carburettor fitted with an automatic choke, the driver must check that the handbrake is applied (on) before the engine is started, as the vehicle could move off unexpectedly, with dire consequences.

Moving Off

Immediately after the correct gear has been selected, the driver must use the mirrors to check the movement and position of any approaching traffic that could make it unsafe to move off. All-round observation should then be taken. He should consider whether to give a signal of his intention to move off — though if

Right:
USE OF THE HANDBRAKE
The driver of this milk float did not apply the handbrake before leaving the vehicle. In consequence the vehicle has rolled back down the road, demolishing a 'keep left' bollard in its path.

given, it provides him with no protection or right of way whatsoever. If there is no immediate danger, no signal is required. The driver should move off only when he is sure it is safe to do so, and not before, so that the manoeuvre will not create potential danger or inconvenience to another road user or pedestrian.

View from the Vehicle

It is the responsibility of the driver to have the best possible observation around the vehicle at all times. A driver sitting in the correct position at the steering wheel must cover the area to the front and sides through an arc of approximately 180°. This can only be achieved by ensuring that the windscreen and other windows are kept clean inside and out. Stickers placed on the windscreen and other windows can obscure a driver's view, and therefore should not be put there. In some vehicles, lucky charms and mascots can be seen hanging from the interior mirror; these swing about in front of the driver, distracting him and obscuring his view of the road, which is potentially dangerous. The mirrors should be properly adjusted so that the best possible view to the rear is gained.

The driver should make sure the windscreen wipers and washers are in good working order. Particles of dust and grit will at times collect on the windscreen, so the washers should be used to assist cleaning before the wipers are used, otherwise the windscreen could get scratched. Furthermore, the bodywork of the vehicle — ie roof supports, door pillars and other parts — can obstruct a driver's view. Adverse weather conditions too can greatly reduce effective observation.

Far left:
MOVING OFF
The driver must use the mirrors before moving off.

Left:
All-round observation must be taken before the decision to move off is made.

3. Car Control

Right:
The Advanced Driver will make sure that all windows, headlamps, auxiliary lamps and lenses are clean.

Below right:
The weather can affect a driver's vision at junctions, and could be a contributory factor in the cause of accidents. A driver who has the glare of the sun in his sight should take all practical precautions to reduce the glare, thus improving his vision before taking the decision to emerge from the junction.

A driver who is approaching a junction with the glare of the sun shining directly in his sight, should use the sun visor, sun glasses or his hand to reduce the glare. Squinting the eyes should be avoided, as this could obscure a vehicle emerging from a side road.

Far right below:
Fog and mist will greatly reduce a driver's view. In this type of situation the driver should lower the respective window(s) and listen for approaching traffic, bearing in mind that fog and mist will deaden the sound of any approaching vehicle until it is close. Thus the driver should be especially diligent in his decision to emerge.

Far left above:
When approaching a junction on a bend with the intention of making a right turn, the driver should, if practicable and safe to do so, position the vehicle towards the centre line, bearing in mind the type and size of vehicle that could approach him.

Above left:
The driver who has a limited view of the road ahead because the severity of the bend and bushes, should lower his window and move his head and body, which will assist him to gain a better view of the road ahead. Having the window down also allows him to listen for other vehicles.

Left:
Only when the driver is absolutely sure it is safe to turn, should he commence to do so.

3. Car Control

4 The System of Car Control

The System of Car Control, as laid down by Lord Cottenham for the Metropolitan Police Driving School in 1937, is a system or drill, each feature of which is considered, in sequence, by the driver at the approach to any hazard. It is the basis upon which the whole technique of good driving is built, and still forms the basis of instruction for police drivers today.

A hazard is anything which contains an element of actual or potential danger. There are three types:

(a) Physical features, such as a junction, roundabout, bend or hill crest.

(b) Those created by the position or movement of other road users.

(c) Those created by variations in road surface or weather conditions.

By definition, every Feature of the System is considered at the approach to any hazard. Only those applicable to the particular circumstances are put into operation but whichever features are selected they must always be in the correct sequence. It is only by constant practice that skill in the application of the System can be acquired.

The System for a Right Turn at a Crossroads

Right:
FEATURE ONE: COURSE
The driver, having seen the junction, will have to change course to that for a right turn. This course is just left of the centre of the road, or into a lane designated for right turn traffic. Therefore the mirrors must be used to check the movements of any following traffic.

Far right:
FEATURE ONE: COURSE
Having used the mirrors to check the movements of any following traffic, a deviation signal should be considered, so that other road users are aware of the driver's intention to change course.

Features of the System

The Features of the System of Car Control are:

1: Course — The driver, having seen the hazard, decides on the correct line of approach. He looks in his mirrors, and if it is necessary to change position to obtain the correct course, he considers a deviation signal.

2: Mirrors, Signals and Speed — The mirrors are again used, and if the intention is to turn right or left at the hazard, consideration must be given to a deviation signal. Any reduction in speed for the hazard will be accomplished at this stage, preceded by a slowing down signal if appropriate.

3: Gear — The correct gear is selected for the speed of the vehicle following application of the second feature.

4: Mirrors and Signals — It is essential to look in the mirrors again and to consider a signal to deviate, if not previously given, or to emphasise an existing deviation signal.

5: Horn — Sound the horn, to give warning of presence, if necessary.

6: Acceleration — The correct degree of acceleration is applied to leave the hazard safely.

It will be seen from the examples given that the System of Car Control is used on the approach to all hazards, although every Feature may not, in fact, need to be applied. Once the driver has learned the System he should practise it continually. He will find through experience that although circumstances may alter on the approach to a hazard, calling for a change of driving plan, the application of the System will become instinctive and form the basis upon which the finer points of driving can be built.

Over the years, many people have criticised Lord Cottenham's technique of driving, but no one has ever bettered his System of Car Control. The opinions and differences on driving a motor vehicle are many, but how many self-opinionated drivers can prove they are the perfect driver? None.

Far left:
FEATURE ONE: COURSE
The correct position for a right turn must be selected. This should be done in plenty of time, having regard to the volume of traffic and speed of approach to the hazard.

Left:
FEATURE ONE: COURSE
The ideal course is just left of the centre of the road.

4. **The System of Car Control**

Right:
FEATURE TWO: MIRRORS, SIGNALS AND SPEED
The mirrors must be used so that the driver is aware of any following traffic. The need for a direction indicator signal should be considered, unless it was used to change course and is therefore still operating. In all probability it will be necessary for the driver to reduce speed: unwanted speed should be achieved by braking, unless only a slight variation in speed is required, in which case deceleration will be sufficient.

Far right:
FEATURE THREE: GEAR
When the speed of the vehicle has been reduced, a gear should be selected to match the road speed of the vehicle. The gear selected should be able to respond readily to variations of accelerator pressure. A vehicle fitted with automatic transmission will select the appropriate gear to match that of the road speed of the vehicle, when the unnecessary road speed has been reduced.

Right:
FEATURE FOUR: MIRRORS AND SIGNALS
When the gear has been selected, the driver should use the mirrors again, as the movement of any following traffic previously observed could have changed, thus creating potential danger. If a direction signal has not been used as yet, it should now be considered. If a signal is in operation, the driver should contemplate the use of an arm signal to confirm his intention to change course.

The System of Car Control for a Right Turn at a Crossroads

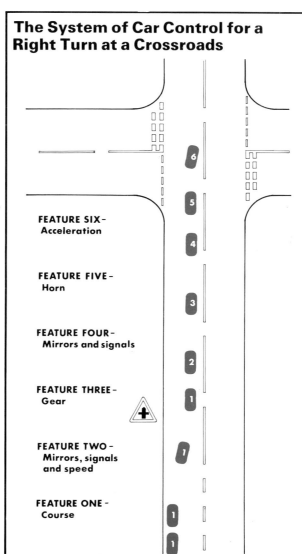

FEATURE SIX – Acceleration

FEATURE FIVE – Horn

FEATURE FOUR – Mirrors and signals

FEATURE THREE – Gear

FEATURE TWO – Mirrors, signals and speed

FEATURE ONE – Course

Far left above:

FEATURE FIVE: HORN
There can be occasions when all reasonable safety precautions have been taken by the driver, but it will still be necessary to draw the attention of another road user or pedestrian, who is obviously vulnerable, to the driver's presence. Therefore an audible signal — from the horn — should be considered, so that the other road user or pedestrian is aware of the driver's presence. The driver must consider that the other road user or pedestrian may have a hearing defect, thus taking nothing for granted.

Far left below:

FEATURE SIX: ACCELERATION
The driver, having seen that it is safe to proceed and having assessed the type and condition of the road surface, should apply a small amount of acceleration to take him round the apex of the corner, thus maintaining the stability of the vehicle. When the vehicle is on a straight course, with a clear road ahead, normal acceleration away from the hazard may be applied. The hazard seen in good time, the driver must use the mirrors so as to be aware of any following traffic. Any deviation in course can then be made safely.

4. The System of Car Control

The System for a Left Turn at a Crossroads

Right:
FEATURE ONE: COURSE
The driver has positioned his vehicle well to the left, the ideal course requiring little or no deviation, as the road ahead can be seen to be clear.

Far right above:
FEATURE TWO: MIRRORS, SIGNALS AND SPEED
Mirrors: The driver should use the mirrors to check the movements and position of any following traffic which was not present when Feature One was applied.

Right:
FEATURE TWO: MIRRORS, SIGNALS AND SPEED
Signals: A direction indicator signal should be considered, so that any other road user approaching the junction will be aware of the driver's intention.

Far right:
FEATURE TWO: MIRRORS, SIGNALS AND SPEED
Speed: In all probability it will be necessary for the driver to reduce speed. This should be achieved by braking, except for slight variation in speed, when deceleration will be sufficient.

Right:

FEATURE THREE: GEARS
When the road speed of the vehicle has been reduced, a gear should be selected to match that of the road speed, at the same time being responsive to slight movement on the accelerator. The driver should look to his right then left, to gain that brief but valuable information of any traffic that could be approaching the junction.

Far right above:

FEATURE FOUR: MIRRORS AND SIGNALS
When the gear has been selected, the driver should use the mirrors to check the situation behind him. If a directional signal has not been used, it should now be considered.

Right:

FEATURE FIVE: HORN
The use of the horn should now be considered, more so if a pedestrian or other road user is not aware of your presence. A vehicle can be seen approaching from the right.

Far right:

FEATURE SIX: ACCELERATION
Gentle acceleration may be applied once the driver is satisfied that the road ahead of him is clear, and that the road surface is safe.

4. The System of Car Control

The System of Car Control for a Left Turn at a Crossroads

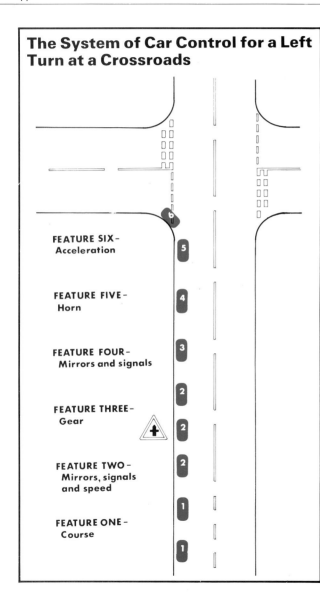

FEATURE SIX –
Acceleration

FEATURE FIVE –
Horn

FEATURE FOUR –
Mirrors and signals

FEATURE THREE –
Gear

FEATURE TWO –
Mirrors, signals
and speed

FEATURE ONE –
Course

Turning Left or Right from a Narrow Road

Left:
The Advanced Driver, looking well ahead, has applied the System in good time. His vision to the right and left is obstructed by a tall hedge and a wall of a barn. The road is narrow, allowing one lane of traffic in each direction, and for that reason the position of the vehicle should be well to the left. The adopted position would be the same for a right turn, because of the reasons stated.

Below left:
The vehicle is less than half its length from the Give Way line. No vision is available to either side, thus the decision to stop has been made. By doing so, additional time has been made available for the driver to check the junction properly before deciding whether to emerge. If in doubt, WAIT.

Left:

TURNING LEFT
This driver is going to turn left at a crossroads. The view to the left is totally obscured by the presence of a tall hedge, therefore no information is available to the driver as to what potential danger lies round the corner. The observant driver will take full advantage from what he can and cannot see to be clear, and therefore be prepared for anything which might happen.

The driver is on the ideal course, requiring little or no deviation from his normal road position. However sharp the corner, do not swing out before turning left, as you will create a potentially dangerous situation for road users who could be passing at the time.

Below left:
With a clear road ahead, position the vehicle well to the left, when turning left.

4. The System of Car Control

5 Roundabouts

Roundabouts

In 1983, 10,500 recorded accidents occurred at or on a roundabout. It is therefore evident that 10,500 road users involved in the accidents did not comply with the advice given in the *Highway Code* because roundabouts are designed to assist traffic flow at junctions, by allowing traffic to enter and leave by different roads, with the minimum of inconvenience or danger.

Roundabouts vary in size and shape from the 'mini' roundabout to the large gyratory complex. They are one-way systems in which traffic circulates in a clockwise direction. When entering a roundabout, the driver should give way to any traffic on his immediate right — unless road markings indicate otherwise — and should keep moving if the way is clear. The System of Car Control should be applied on the approach and entering the roundabout, thus allowing time to react to faults that can be committed by other road users. The 'Give Way' rule at roundabouts was introduced in 1964.

Far left below:
This aerial view of a large gyratory complex shows a two-way traffic system, allowing double the volume of traffic to use the roundabout. The 'Give Way' rule, to traffic on the right, applies.

Below left:
The configuration of mini roundabouts may seem confusing at first sight. The System of Car Control, if applied on the approach, will enable the driver to negotiate the roundabout in safety.

Right:
This lamp post, erected on an island on a mini-roundabout, encourages drivers to adopt a correct course and reduce speed.

Far right above:
Like any other roundabout, vehicle positioning is of the utmost importance. A driver should go round the white blob — not over it as so many drivers do, as can be seen by the tyre marks.

Far right:
A driver catching up with other traffic on a roundabout should hold back, and wait for the other drivers to decide their course.

5. Roundabouts

Above right:
Due to the speed limit of the road, and the acute angle of the approach to the roundabout, roadside markers have been placed to warn drivers of the sharp deviation of route. The posts are black and white, with oblong amber reflectors.

Right:
The driver *on* the roundabout must look to his left at the approach road before the exit he intends to take. This is because there are drivers who approach a roundabout too fast, and look to the right too late, emerging into the driver's path before attempting to give way.

Roundabouts: Straight Ahead

The driver, having seen the hazard, will look in the mirrors before applying Feature One, and therefore be aware of following traffic should a change of course have to be made.

Above left:

FEATURE ONE: COURSE
Unless conditions dictate otherwise, the position on the approach should be to the nearside. If practically possible, the chosen line should be maintained through the roundabout.

Far left:

FEATURE TWO: MIRRORS, SIGNALS AND SPEED
With the vehicle in the correct position on the road, the driver must use the mirrors; if traffic is following, a slowing down signal should be considered. Generally, it will be necessary to slow down for the roundabout, bearing in mind the need to give way to traffic from the immediate right.

Left:

FEATURE THREE: GEARS
A gear should be selected that is most responsive to the accelerator, should the need to use it arise.

5. Roundabouts

Right:

FEATURE FOUR: MIRRORS AND SIGNALS

Immediately after the gear change has been made, the driver should use the mirrors to check if the situation behind has changed. A deviation signal would not be required, but an arm signal should be considered to emphasise the intention to slow down, if not previously given.

Below right:

FEATURE FIVE: HORN

The use of the horn should now be considered, with particular consideration for pedestrians, but it must not be used in the belief that it will ensure a safe passage.

Far right below:

FEATURE SIX: ACCELERATION

Acceleration should be considered, and if necessary applied to drive the vehicle through the roundabout. The features of the ground and the movement of other vehicles must be dealt with as the situation occurs.

Generally, it is undesirable to increase speed, unless the momentum of the vehicle is inadequate for the prevailing conditions.

Roundabouts: Turning Right

Far left:
FEATURE ONE: COURSE
The driver, having seen the hazard, will look in the mirrors for any following traffic, and if necessary a right-turn directional indicator signal should be given. When safe to do so, the vehicle should be positioned on the ideal course, just left of the centre of the road.

Left:
FEATURE TWO: MIRRORS, SIGNALS AND SPEED
The mirrors must be used and a direction indicator signal should be considered. The driver will in all probability have to reduce speed, to comply with the legal requirement to give way to traffic from the immediate right. The driver has used the mirrors, is signalling his intention to turn right by means of the direction indicator, and is reducing speed by proper use of the brakes.

Far left:
FEATURE THREE: GEARS
A gear should be selected that is most responsive to the accelerator, should the situation change.

Left:
FEATURE FOUR: MIRRORS AND SIGNALS
Immediately after the gear change has been made, the driver should use the mirrors to check if the situation behind has changed. If a directional signal has not been used it should be considered at this stage; if being used, it should continue in operation through the roundabout.

5. Roundabouts

Right:
FEATURE FIVE: HORN
The use of the horn should now be considered.

Far right:
FEATURE SIX: ACCELERATION
Acceleration is considered, bearing in mind the contours of the roads and the close proximity of any hazards. Generally, an increase in speed is undesirable, provided that the momentum of the vehicle is adequate for the prevailing conditions.

Below right:
NEGOTIATING THE ROUNDABOUT
When opposite the junction before the one by which the driver is intending to leave, a left direction indicator signal should be considered, if it will be of use to another road user.

Far right:
NEGOTIATING THE ROUNDABOUT
When leaving the roundabout, acceleration should be applied as for a left turn.

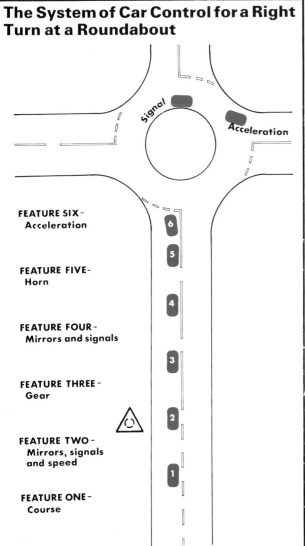

The System of Car Control for a Right Turn at a Roundabout

Signal

Acceleration

FEATURE SIX -
Acceleration

FEATURE FIVE -
Horn

FEATURE FOUR -
Mirrors and signals

FEATURE THREE -
Gear

FEATURE TWO -
Mirrors, signals
and speed

FEATURE ONE -
Course

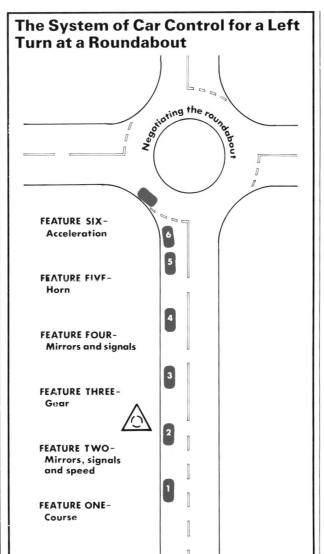

The System of Car Control for a Left Turn at a Roundabout

Negotiating the roundabout

FEATURE SIX -
Acceleration

FEATURE FIVE -
Horn

FEATURE FOUR -
Mirrors and signals

FEATURE THREE -
Gear

FEATURE TWO -
Mirrors, signals
and speed

FEATURE ONE -
Course

5. Roundabouts

Roundabouts: Turning Left

The driver, having seen the hazard, will look in the mirrors for any following traffic before applying Feature One, and will therefore be aware of following traffic should a change of course have to be made.

Right:
FEATURE ONE: COURSE
The driver should position the vehicle to the nearside, requiring little or no deviation from his normal road position.

Below right:
FEATURE TWO: MIRRORS, SIGNALS AND SPEED
The mirrors must be used and a direction indicator signal should be considered. The driver will in all probability have to reduce speed, having due regard to the requirement to give way to traffic from the immediate right. The driver has used the mirrors, is signalling his intention to turn left by means of the direction indicator, and is reducing speed by proper use of the brakes.

Far right:
FEATURE THREE: GEARS
A gear should be selected that is most responsive to the accelerator, should the need arise.

Right:
FEATURE FOUR: MIRRORS AND SIGNALS
Immediately after the gear change has been made, the driver should use the mirrors to check if the situation behind has changed. If a directional signal has not been used it should be considered at this stage; if being used, it should continue in operation through the roundabout.

Far right:
FEATURE FIVE: HORN
The use of the horn should now be considered.

Below right:
FEATURE SIX: ACCELERATION
Acceleration is considered, bearing in mind the contours and surface of the road, and close proximity of any hazards. Generally an increase in speed is undesirable, providing the momentum of the vehicle is adequate for the prevailing conditions.

Far right:
NEGOTIATING THE ROUNDABOUT
The hazards presented by the features of the ground and the movement of other vehicles must be dealt with, as the situation occurs, by using the appropriate Features of the System. This driver is in the correct position on the road when leaving the roundabout.

6 Road Signs, Observation and Signals

Traffic Signs and Road Markings

It is believed that the history and use of traffic signs in the United Kingdom originated with the Romans, they being the first people in Britain to make use of 'traffic signs' by marking their roads with stones called 'Milliaries'. In all probability the distance of 'one mile' originated from their word Milliary, although the actual measurement differs.

Since the Romans, the history of signposts is somewhat obscure. The General Turnpike Act of 1773 imposed on the Turnpike Trusts the obligation of setting up and maintaining signposts on all the roads under their charge. The appearance of the bicycle in the latter part of the 19th century, created a new hazard to other road users. Some local authorities erected their own cautions signs at the top of steep hills, thus warning cyclists of the danger when descending a hill.

The advent of the first horseless carriage came in 1895, and by 1899 electric tramcars and motor omnibuses were to be seen in

Right:
In some areas Rumble Strips, at times combined with white lines, are laid at the edge of the road to warn road users of the potential danger of ill-defined verges.

Far right:
Horse Droppings: an obvious clue to potential danger, but how many drivers take heed of the warning?

London, creating problems in streets which were not designed for them. They contributed to the congestion and chaos in the centre of London. In 1903 the Motor Car Act authorised the raising of the speed limit for motor vehicles from 12mph to 20mph, at the same time introducing a system of licensing for vehicle drivers. The accident injury rate in London at that time was running at an average of over 10,000 accidents per year.

For the first 30 years of this century, motoring organisations had the task of signposting the roads in the United Kingdom. After World War 1, white lines began to appear on the roads of Britain; during the 1920s their use spread rapidly. In the 1930s, white lines were used as 'Stop' lines at road junctions controlled either by police or by traffic lights, for marking the course to be taken at bends, junctions and corners, and for indicating the proximity of refuges and other obstacles in the carriageway. In 1934, reflecting studs (cat's-eyes) came into use.

New signs introduced in 1933 continued in use until the early 1960s, when the current system of road signs was adopted. By 1965 all the 'regulatory' signs giving commands or prohibitions were used in the United Kingdom, thus complying with the European practice on traffic signs.

This brief history of traffic signs and road markings confirms the fact that with ever increasing traffic volumes, the need for more of the informative traffic signs is of paramount importance. The variety of signs, signals and road markings we have today convey their information quickly and accurately, but to be of any use the driver must understand the message they give, otherwise lives could be in danger.

Traffic signs and road markings, combined with signals given by other road users, are the language of the road. It is disturbing but true that the average road user does not see or understand the majority of road signs provided for his guidance. Unless a diligent effort is made by road users to improve their knowledge of the information given by traffic signs and road markings, they will be the cause of accidents.

The Advanced Driver, having seen the sign and understood its meaning, will look well ahead giving himself time and opportunity to assess the situation to which the sign refers, and formulate a safe driving plan.

6. Road Signs, Observation and Signals

Traffic Signs

There are many traffic signs, ordering, warning and informing road users, and thereby improving traffic flow and road safety. The provision of new signs is a continuous process, taking into account developments in other areas of motoring. Naturally, traffic signs include those for the safety of pedestrians.

Above right:
The message given by the four traffic signs and the hazard lines is clear. The Advanced Driver will implement a safe driving plan in good time, anticipating the obvious dangers.

Right:
A hump bridge can hide many dangers. A good driver will reduce speed well before reaching the bridge, thus being in a position to stop his vehicle within the distance he can see to be clear.

Far right:
The observant driver will position his vehicle in the appropriate lane for the direction he intends to travel, well before reaching the road he is going to join. Late road positioning is the cause of many accidents.

Left:
The traffic sign warns the driver of the danger that can be seen ahead. On a railway crossing the Advanced Driver will consider and apply each feature of the System as that for going straight ahead at a crossroads. The amber lights and audible warning, followed by flashing red lights, warn that a train is approaching and that the barriers are about to come down. YOU MUST STOP.

6. Road Signs, Observation and Signals

Above right:
The traffic sign warns the driver of a hidden dip (dead ground). A driver must comply with the road markings: in so doing he will increase his margin of safety. There have been many fatal accidents due to drivers ignoring the information given by traffic signs and road markings.

Right:
Certain types of vehicle are prohibited from using some roads, for numerous and often obvious reasons.

Far left:
As seen here, Tower Bridge, London, has automatic traffic signals to control traffic when the bridge has to be raised.

Left:
A STOP sign is a mandatory sign and is to be complied with; failure to do so is an offence. Regardless of the fact that no other traffic can be seen at the time, it is no excuse for not complying with the information given by the sign.

Below left:
There are some drivers, such as the cyclist, who do not know the shape, and/or colour, of a NO ENTRY sign: thus they cannot be aware of the danger or offence being committed by failing to comply with the sign.
July 1931 saw the introduction of 68 sets of automatic traffic signals at 17 junctions in Oxford Street, London, thus becoming part of the first flexible progressive system to be introduced. Since that date, automatic light signals are being used to control traffic at numerous locations where there is danger or potential danger. A red flashing light, for example, is used to control traffic at:

- **Fire stations**
- **Motorways**
- **Level crossings**
- **Ferries**
- **Cattle crossings**
- **Swing or opening bridges**
- **Tunnels**
- **Airfields**

6. Road Signs, Observation and Signals

Road Markings

Right:
Because of the road works blocking the road, a driver will have little choice but to go round them. Great care must be taken before proceeding over the hatched area, as approaching vehicles and traffic turning right have the right of way. Only when it is safe can progress be made.

Below right:
In some areas, special lanes have been reserved for buses, to maintain a scheduled public service. Unless the bus lane is physically separated from the rest of the carriageway by an island, vehicles may enter the bus lane to stop to load or unload, but only at times when there is no restriction on loading. A Bus Lane is not designed for impatient motorist to pass a queue of traffic.

Far right:
A box junction has been designed where there is a likelihood that traffic could block a road junction. Do not enter the box unless your exit is clear, except when a right turn has to be taken and you are prevented from doing so by oncoming traffic or other stationary vehicles waiting to complete a right turn.

Box markings at junctions were introduced in 1964.

Left:
This driver, aware of the meaning of the road markings, has positioned his vehicle in the deceleration lane designated for traffic turning right. Drivers should not enter the hatched area except in an emergency.

Far left below:
This driver has made a slight deviation from his normal position towards the nearside, taking up a safe position for a left turn.

Below left:
The driver of this vehicle has parked indiscriminately, having no regard for other road users and therefore creating a potentially dangerous situation.

6. Road Signs, Observation and Signals

Above right:
A driver should not rely on what he can see to be true, as this example of a hazard line proves. A driver with poor powers of observation and concentration, and tired, would in all probability have an accident; more so at night or driving at an excessive speed for the conditions prevailing.

Right:
There will be times when road markings are not visible. That is no excuse to ignore the situation: the driver should reduce speed and look for possible clues to inform or guide him. For example, even though the road surface is covered with snow, it is still an offence to park or wait within the zig-zag areas on both sides of the crossing. Other aspects of the law relating to pedestrian crossings also must be complied with in these circumstances.

Temporary Traffic Signs

For one reason or another it might not be feasible to place, or the site might not warrant, a permanent traffic sign. Therefore a temporary sign is placed by the roadside, informing road users of the danger or hazard. Whatever traffic sign is shown, it should be exploited to the driver's advantage.

Far left above:
This warning sign with a message (Try Your Brakes) has been placed because of flood water. The message is clear: therefore do it.

Above left:
The temporary traffic sign informs the driver that there is a failure of light signals such that the junction is uncontrolled. Every precaution should be taken on the approach to and at the junction, because not all other road users might be aware of the message given by the sign.

Left:
These additional traffic signs are placed to inform road users of the condition of the road surface. Speed should be reduced to avoid damage to the driver's vehicle, and to that of others.

6. Road Signs, Observation and Signals

Road Observation

Good standards of health and vision, clean and clear windows, and the ability to concentrate are the factors needed to obtain and maintain good road observation. These numerous factors, when combined, will enable the driver to see the detailed information required to assess a situation and formulate and execute a driving plan.

Concentration

Concentration and road observation are linked, for without the former the latter will not be accomplished. It is a fact that many drivers are unable to concentrate with complete mastery for any period of time: attention wanders and concentration fails. With this lack of self-discipline the driver puts his own and others' safety at risk.

Driving Plans

The expert driver, looking well ahead and making proper use of the mirrors, is aware of the constantly changing situation around him at all times. Driving plans and decisions are based on three deciding factors.

(1) What Can Be Seen: Decisions on the use of speed can only be made when the driver has an unobstructed view of the road ahead. It must be borne in mind at all times that he must be able to stop his vehicle in the distance he can see to be clear, having due regard to the type of road surface at the time.

(2) What Cannot Be Seen: The view of the road is obstructed by a bridge on a bend; difficulties could arise from areas that the driver cannot see to be clear, therefore the System of Car Control is applied and road speed thereby adjusted.

(3) Circumstances Which May Reasonably Be Expected To Develop: Here a funfair in a rural high street, a junction on the left combined with the possibility of pedestrians emerging between the side shows and on to the zebra crossing, and approaching traffic, all contribute to the need for a driver to be able to stop his vehicle in the distance he can see to be clear.

Below:

WHAT CAN BE SEEN
By looking well ahead, the expert driver will gain from the information given by the traffic sign. With the potential dangers seen in good time he can formulate a driving plan and leave nothing to chance.

Far right below:

WHAT CANNOT BE SEEN
A defensive attitude of mind must be applied to avoid mistakes made by others, thus avoiding potential accidents.

Left:
CIRCUMSTANCES WHICH MAY REASONABLY BE EXPECTED TO DEVELOP
Concentration and anticipation will give the observant driver time to react from the mistakes made by others.

Far left:
ROAD OBSERVATION
The information given by the traffic sign and situation is clear. Effective observation of approaching traffic can be taken from this position. In this situation the driver will have to cross the double white lines to pass the hazard, so long as no danger is created to approaching traffic while passing the hazard. If in doubt, WAIT.

Left:
To stop in this position is ludicrous and dangerous, but many drivers do and then try to edge out, creating danger to themselves and others.

6. Road Signs, Observation and Signals

Right:
The driver's view on the approach to this right hand bend is obscured by the tall hedge, but by looking to the right the driver will see the top of a bus approaching the bend. If the driver did not use his powers of observation, the bus would not have been seen.

Below right:
This driver is getting a brief but valuable view of the road ahead by looking through the break in the hedge. The average driver would class his observation totally obscured by the hedge and trees.

Left:

The horse, passing the time of day while standing in a position such that a driver's view of the bends — particularly from a low sports car — is obstructed. Note too the advisory speed limit sign which relates to the newly laid road surface of loose stone chippings. Due to the restricted view of the bends, and new road surface, the defensive driver should reduce speed for (1) the restricted view of the bends; (2) so that the horse is not frightened when it is passed; and (3) for the loose road surface. When the horse has been passed, it would be justifiable to sound the horn as a warning to any other road user who cannot be seen at the time and place.

Left:

This irregular and undulating road has adequate traffic signs, informing the driver of the prevailing hazard. The driver, having applied the System, will have positioned his vehicle well to the left on the approach, so that maximum visibility is gained.

Above right:
At this point an approaching vehicle can be seen: therefore pull up and let it pass. When the road is clear, proceed. Just before reaching the top of the bridge, the horn should be used to warn any approaching traffic of your presence. The observant driver will notice a sharp left bend beginning from the top of the bridge. Note also the mirrors that have been vandalised and thus rendered useless.

The need for advanced observation cannot be stressed enough, because a driver negotiates numerous different types of bend of varying severity on a journey. When the driver has made an assessment of the bend and of additional hazards, then the speed and position can be adjusted for maximum safety.

Right:
Ahead, a train looks as though it is crossing the road — or is there a bridge? This is a mystery if other information has not been gleaned in good time.

Above left:
By taking full advantage of views across fields and through hedges, fences and walls, an approaching vehicle can be seen by a driver. The course of the road illustrated can be seen by the position of the telegraph poles.

Left:
Looking between the heavy goods vehicle and the fence, a view of the road ahead can be obtained. Note the thoughtless motorist who has stopped his vehicle in a dangerous place to have a chat, thus committing three offences.

6. Road Signs, Observation and Signals

Adverse Weather

Allowances should always be made for the mistakes of other road users. It is unsafe to assume that another driver will react correctly to any given situation; he may have passed his driving test only that day, or be driving a strange or defective vehicle. He may be a naturally aggressive or thoughtless driver, or attempting to drive beyond his capabilities for the prevailing conditions in order to keep an urgent appointment.

It is surprising — but true — that the average driver is not aware of one essential fact: he should always be in a position to stop his vehicle well within the distance he sees to be clear. Horrific pile-ups in mist, fog and smoke prove that this rule has not been applied. It has been said that concentration and road observation are very closely related, for without the former, success in the latter cannot possibly be achieved. The value and assessment of what is seen allows a driving plan to be formulated.

When fog is seen, the Advanced Driver will apply Feature Two of the System of Car Control (Mirrors, Signals and Speed). The headlights (with the beam dipped) and rear fog lamps should be switched on, and the mirrors are used to check the movement and position of following traffic. An arm signal ('I intend to slow down or stop') should be considered to inform following traffic of the intention to slow down. Speed is reduced by deceleration or proper application of the brakes, and a safe following distance maintained from the vehicle in front, thus giving the driver and other road users time and distance to pull up well within the distance that can be seen to be clear. It cannot be stressed too strongly that this procedure must be implemented in good time, and not when it is too late or not at all, which is often the case. Some drivers rely on warning lights to inform them of danger, instead of using their eyes to see the danger. It should be borne in mind that fog can form randomly at any place, quite possibly where warning lights are no sited.

When driving on stretches of road affected by heavy rain, a curtain of spray from other vehicles will reduce further a driver's view of the road ahead. In such conditions the driver must use the headlamps with the beam dipped, thereby informing other road users of his presence. A driver, aware he is catching up with another vehicle, must decide either to adjust his speed and

Right:
In fog KEEP YOUR DISTANCE. Headlamps with the beam dipped and rear fog lamps must be used. Windscreen wipers assist to keep the windscreen clear; but to do so, they and the washers must be in proper working order.

follow at a safe distance while it makes reasonable progress, or overtake at the first opportunity. If the decision to overtake is made, the mirrors must be used to check the movements of any following traffic, and he should consider the need for a signal before changing course. The flashing of headlights should be used to draw attention to your presence on the road when the decision to overtake is made.

It must be borne in mind that the road situation can change at any moment — for example, a high sided vehicle could be affected by cross wind, or could pull out to overtake. On a two-lane motorway, heavy goods vehicles are permitted to use the overtaking lane, but are prohibited from using the third or fourth lane where such lanes exist.

The speed of the vehicle to be overtaken must be considered, as the higher speed required to overtake could induce 'aqua planing', particularly if the tread depth of the tyres is getting near the minimum legal limit. On a badly drained road surface at a speed in excess of 50mph, the driver's ability and the type, condition and limitations of the vehicle must all be considered before the decision to overtake can be made. If there is any doubt, the driver should not attempt to overtake.

Above left:
Heavy rain combined with a curtain of spray being thrown up by the heavy goods vehicle (which is not using lamps or rear fog lamps and is thus not complying with the *Highway Code*) make it difficult for the average driver to judge the speed and distance.

Left:
A good driver is one who looks well ahead, recognises any change in road surface conditions, and applies the correct values of braking, acceleration and steering. The lane that has been cleared of snow should be used, and the potentially dangerous snow-covered lanes avoided. Adverse weather conditions, no matter what the cause, may demand a drastic reduction in speed to keep within the bounds of safety. Where ice is present four times the normal stopping distance must be allowed, therefore the distance from the vehicle in front must be extended, to equal the distance for stopping.

6. Road Signs, Observation and Signals

Right:
A lay-by is an ideal place to pull in and have a rest from driving.

Below right:
There are many places where a driver can pull in to have refreshment and freshen up.

Fatigue

Travelling at high speed requires total concentration and mental alertness, and driving a considerable distance without stopping (but within the law), possibly combined with night-time dazzle and ever-changing conditions of visibility, will result in tiredness. Good ventilation and driving with a window open can assist to delay the effects. However, when the driver feels his driving skills are deteriorating, he should pull up at a suitable place and freshen up. This can be achieved by washing his face, taking refreshment (hot drink and food) then going for a walk to improve his circulation. When he is refreshed, it should be safe for him to proceed with his journey.

If the driver is totally exhausted there is no option, in the interest of safety, but to park the vehicle, book in at a hotel and gain a good night's rest.

Smoke

For many years farmers have been burning stubble at the end of the harvest; apart from other problems which arise, smoke from any source creates potential danger to the motorist. If the wind should change course, the smoke could blow across the road, thus reducing visibility drastically.

Observation at Junctions

The definition of a hazard is anything which contains an element of actual or potential danger. This applies to junctions of whatever type, therefore they must be approached with caution. Like any hazard, every feature of the System must be considered at the approach to a junction, and the Features applied must be relevant to the particular situation. Whichever Features of the System are selected, they must always be in the correct sequence, at the right time and place, then a systematic approach to the hazard will be made, thus leaving nothing to chance.

To give some idea of the potential danger that could be at or near a junction, in 1983 there were 145,800 injury accidents that occurred at or within 20m of a junction. The drivers involved can tell how the accidents happened, but not always why.

For many years it was considered that one of the most difficult and potentially dangerous manoeuvres for a driver was a right turn at a crossroads, due to the presence of other road users approaching the junction from three other directions. There were 29,200 injury accidents at crossroads, but statistics for 1983, the year to which these accident figures relate, inform us that there were 82,200 injury accidents at or within 20m of 'T' or staggered junctions, which shows that these types of junction contain a higher element of accident risk than crossroads.

There are many reasons why accidents can and do occur at junctions, and there are various aspects about junctions worthy of further detail here. For example, the Advanced Driver will assess what he can see once the information given by the traffic sign has been observed — ie, crossroads, 'T' or other type of junction — and the movement of any vehicular and pedestrian traffic recognised. As the driver approaches the junction, he should be able to see clearly into the road which he is going to join or cross. If for one reason or another his view is obscured, he should move his vehicle slowly forward, at the same time looking right, left and right again; only when he is sure it is safe to do so, should he proceed. If there is any doubt, he should wait.

Effective observation, and taking appropriate action on what can and cannot be seen, is of paramount importance in preventing an accident. By using hearing, additional assistance can be gained by the sound of approaching traffic that cannot be seen — more so when the road surface is wet. This can only be achieved if the relevant window(s) is down, the radio-cassette player is not in use, and passengers are not talking.

A driver, when sitting in a normal driving position in a saloon car, will on average have a view of the road ahead, to his rear and to either side from about 4ft above the ground. Therefore, any objects in the vicinity which are above 4ft high will hide potential danger.

A driver's zone of vision on the approach to, and at, a junction can be obscured by many things — street furniture like lamp-posts, keep-left bollards on a central refuge and traffic signs, and other fixtures such as railings, telegraph poles,

postboxes, hedges and shrubs. Even a pedestrian walking on the pavement can obscure a driver's view of the road he is going to join. There are certain parts of a vehicle's bodywork that also obstruct a driver's view — roof supports, door pillars, etc — thus the driver will have to move his head or body to gain a better and unrestricted view of the road he is going to join.

The weather too can impair vision from inside a car. If the driver omits to keep his vehicle well ventilated on a cold or wet day, the windows will mist up, thereby greatly reducing his all-round vision. During the winter, vehicles have been driven with the windows covered in frost, ice and snow, and some drivers make no conscious effort to improve the situation until the heater and heated rear window disperse it, which is lazy and dangerous. On the other hand, on a sunny day the windows can be clean and clear, but the glare of the sun shining in the driver's eyes will reduce his field of vision. To combat this, the use of the sun visor or sunglasses will help to reduce the glare.

Whatever the circumstances at a junction, it is the driver's responsibility to act sensibly on what he can and cannot see to be clear. Some drivers look right, left and right again on the approach to or at a junction — and then emerge into the path of an approaching vehicle. Often the reason they take this dangerous action is because they do not make effective use of what they see, or do not take appropriate action: ie, to wait at the junction until it is safe to emerge into the road which they are going to cross or join.

A driver should never assume anything at a junction, and should not emerge until he is completely sure it is safe to proceed. Another contributory factor to the cause of accidents at junctions is that many drivers either look too early or too late. If they look too early they could in all probability be in the wrong

position to be able to see what vehicles are approaching, because their visibility on the approach can be very limited for reasons previously mentioned. At the other extreme, if they look too late, they see an approaching vehicle too late, particularly if their speed is in excess of that for the necessary stopping distance.

There have been occasions when observation has been taken at the right time and place, but some drivers, due to lack of concentration, carelessness, fatigue, inexperience, poor visibility or even defective eyesight, underestimate the speed and distance of an approaching vehicle. Some drivers are under the impression that the smaller the approching vehicle, the farther away it must be. To some extent this is true, but not always. A classic example of this is the motorcycle. Motorbikes are a third of the size of a saloon car, which is why there are so many bike-related accidents at junctions. The average driver is looking for other cars and commercial vehicles, and it is possible to miss the approaching motorcyclist.

THINK BIKE Before Emerging

Modern motorcycles and mopeds are much faster than their predecessors, so do not underestimate the speed and distance of an approaching motorcyclist: many drivers have done so and in consequence emerged into a junction, causing serious injury or a fatal accident. Not all motorcyclists help to make themselves more visible to drivers by wearing brightly coloured clothing, belt or tabard which provide fluorescent day-time brightness and night-time reflective brilliance. Indeed, some motorcyclists do not even drive with their headlamps on during daylight hours.

Motorcyclists are much more vulnerable to the elements, dangerous road surfaces and other potential dangers than car drivers. Some drivers do not appreciate or are not even aware of these problems. It has been explained how the different types of road surface and other factors can affect and determine the overall stopping distance of a vehicle at a given speed. Motorcycles and mopeds take a greater distance to stop than a saloon car or van, even more so in adverse weather conditions and on inferior road surfaces.

It *must* be appreciated that the overall size of a motorcyclist and motorcycle is about one third of the size of a car — easily missed if effective observation is not taken, and easily hit if effective action is not taken once it has been seen.

The Government is trying to reduce accidents involving the two-wheeled road user; it is the responsibility of every driver to make his contribution to prevent road accidents occurring.

OBSCURED OBSERVATION

These are some typical situations which show how easy it is to misjudge or fail to see another road user if correct and effective observation is not taken. There are drivers who glance instead of looking right, left and right again before emerging into a junction. The lazy driver is a potential accident.

Above left:
A driver who does not take effective observation would in all probability not see the moped. If the driver should emerge into the junction, an accident could occur.

Left:
If practicably possible, a driver should pull up where he can see any approaching traffic, and not in this position. Can you see a motorcyclist?

6. Road Signs, Observation and Signals

Right:
In 1983, 10,400 recorded accidents occurred at the junction of a private driveway or entrance and the public highway. Extra care should be applied when a driver has to reverse his vehicle on to the highway from a private driveway or entrance.

Below right:
This row of trees obstructs a driver's view, therefore he should position his vehicle with caution, so that an unobstructed view is obtained.

Far right:
The Advanced Driver will make full use of the shop windows, looking for reflections of approaching vehicles which would not otherwise be seen.

Turning Right at Traffic Lights

The conventional way for a driver to turn right at a junction controlled by traffic lights is that when an opposing vehicle is also turning right, the driver should pass the approaching vehicle offside-to-offside, completing the manoeuvre when safe to do so. If the design of the junction makes it impractical for offside-to-offside passing, or the driver of the opposing vehicle indicates his intention by his road position, or traffic signs and road markings indicate it, the driver may have to pass the opposing vehicle nearside-to-nearside. In these situations it must be borne in mind that a driver's view of oncoming traffic can be obscured should a vehicle be turning right at the same time. The driver should take every precaution before proceeding into the area of road that cannot be seen to be clear.

Left:
Turning offside-to-offside is effective until some selfish drivers bunch up, when it becomes unworkable due to inconsiderate driving.

Far left below:
As can be seen by the road markings, the driver is directed to turn nearside-to-nearside. At the given time, the driver can see approaching traffic.

Below left:
A driver turning right nearside-to-nearside in this situation would have his view of approaching traffic and the traffic signals obscured by the commercial vehicle, so every precaution should be taken before emerging into the area of road that cannot be seen to be clear.

6. Road Signs, Observation and Signals

Right:

When emerging from a junction which is on a bend, the driver should look right, left and right again, continuously. The vehicle should be moved slowly forward at the same time, provided it is safe to do so. In this situation it could take only one second for the motorcyclist to appear from the driver's blind area caused by the tree and shrubs; it is a good example of where a driver could listen for approaching traffic.

Far right above:

The driver has applied the System, giving the cyclist precedence before turning left and crossing the cycle track.

Right:

The motorcyclist has emerged into the path of the 'L' driver, creating a potentially dangerous situation. It must be borne in mind that a driver should, where practicably possible, look into the side roads as they are approached, thus being aware of any additional danger.

Above left:
When waiting to emerge from a junction, do not assume a vehicle approaching from the right with its left-hand direction indicator operating *will* turn left. A driver should wait for supporting evidence — ie, a considerable reduction in speed and/or a change in course — before moving out.

Left:
The minibus is approaching a junction, signalling with its left-hand direction indicator. To all intents and purposes the average driver would assume the minibus is going to turn left.
The intention of the driver of the minibus is to pull up on the left just after the junction. There have been numerous accidents at or near a junction due to improper use of signals.

6. Road Signs, Observation and Signals

Observation in Traffic

In town driving, where traffic is really heavy and slow, the driver can position his vehicle to gain a view of the road ahead. When following a commercial vehicle, it is more difficult to make an accurate forecast of traffic movement ahead because of the very limited view available.

Right:
By following a vehicle of this type in such a position as this, the driver's view is very restricted.

Far right:
By making a slight deviation in road position, or dropping back, a driver will obtain a view of the traffic ahead. Therefore traffic movement and other potential dangers will be seen.

Driving Plans

Right:
The Advanced Driver who applies the System for a right turn will have observed the brewer's dray in good time, thus making sure he can complete the manoeuvre safely. The driver should always have a good view of the road into which he is going to turn before starting a manoeuvre, otherwise a potentially dangerous situation could occur. If in any doubt, he should wait until he is sure it is safe to proceed.

Left:
There are many drivers who approach a junction applying their own or no system. In so doing they fail to appreciate the need to take up a progressive position as they exit from the junction.

Far left below:
One problem many drivers create is incorrect positioning after a right turn, as shown here. The average driver will in all probability position the vehicle for normal driving. In this situation the driver's view of the road ahead is obstructed by the heavy goods vehicle, which has not been taken into consideration.

Left:
The Advanced Driver will assess and recognise potential danger before commencing the right turn. By positioning the vehicle correctly after turning right, as shown here, his view will not be obscured by the heavy goods vehicle. Therefore he will see the approaching vehicle in good time, thus giving himself time to act.

6. Road Signs, Observation and Signals

Right:
When joining a road that has a 60mph speed limit, remember that an approaching vehicle travelling at 60mph would cover distance at 88ft/sec. It is of the utmost importance that the speed and distance of any approaching vehicle is assessed correctly, otherwise a fatal accident could occur. Remember to look right, left and right again before deciding to move forward.

Below right:
When approaching a junction, the driver should appreciate that the length of a bus or heavy goods vehicle may cause the driver to cut the corner due to the road layout. In such a case it is good sense to hold back.

Far right:
The driver of the heavy goods vehicle has positioned his vehicle for a left turn. When the turn is made, the heavy goods vehicle, by virtue of its length, will restrict the space on his nearside, and a vehicle on his left could well be placed in a dangerous situation with no escape; again it is good sense to hold back, thus allowing the articulated vehicle to complete the turn safely.

Dead Ground

There are two types of dead ground, both of which hide potential danger: (1) That caused by a road having a steep dip, such that approaching vehicles will not be seen until near the summit; (2) That caused by a hump back bridge, where oncoming vehicles will not be seen until reaching the crest. The expert driver will take into account what cannot be seen and will therefore approach the hazard at such a speed that he can stop his vehicle within the distance he can see to be clear. By doing so, he will prevent himself from becoming involved in an accident.

Left:
A STEEP DIP
A vehicle is coming out of the dip.

Below left:
HUMP BACK BRIDGE
A motorcyclist is reaching the crest.

6. Road Signs, Observation and Signals

Top right:
In slow moving traffic the driver must use the nearside mirror. If one is not fitted, he should look over his left shoulder for cyclists that could be creeping up on the nearside, before a left turn is made.

Above right:
When a vehicle is following too closely — and thus unsafely — it is of the utmost importance that the driver is aware of the situation, before applying the brakes or changing direction.

Right:
A driver can make sure it is safe to change course by using the offside mirror, thereby being able to see the road that is obscured by the following vehicle.

Driving Mirrors

The Advanced Driver is aware of the situation behind as well as to the front of him, by making proper use of the mirrors. This can only be achieved by self-discipline and practice. There are drivers who look in the mirrors, but do not make effective use of what they see well before signalling, changing direction, slowing down and stopping, thus committing a dangerous act or offence.

The proper use of the mirrors at the right time and place is part of the System of Car Control: if a driver omits to use the mirrors at a given time or place, the System is incomplete and could be dangerous.

'Drivers' Signals

Signals are the means by which drivers warn other road users of their intention and presence. There are three types of visible signal fitted to every new car: the direction indicator signals, stop lamps and headlamps; and the driver's arm signal makes a fourth. They are the language of the road, and are the only visible way drivers can inform other road users and pedestrians of their intention and presence.

To be of any use, signals must be given clearly as illustrated in the *Highway Code*, and at the right time and place — ie Feature Two of the System of Car Control. If no other road user or pedestrian is in sight then a signal is superfluous. However, it should be considered again at Feature Four of the System.

A signal gives a warning, not an instruction, and gives no right of way whatsoever to carry out an intended action. Too many serious accidents are caused by drivers and motorcyclists who signal their intention to carry out a manoeuvre without taking rear observation before changing course, regardless of the position and speed of other road users who could be following or overtaking them at the time.

Stop Lamps

The stop lamps are fitted to the rear of the vehicle and are illuminated when the foot brake pedal is pressed. They provide a useful signal in circumstances where advance warning should be given of the intention to slow down or stop. It must be borne in mind that the stop lamps will not illuminate until the brakes are applied; it is also of utmost importance that the mirrors are used before applying the footbrake.

Headlamps

The flashing of headlights should not be used for signalling in daylight unless in lieu of a horn warning for overtaking at speed on motorways, dual carriageways and other fast roads: on these the application of the System and, therefore, the warning of approach will be earlier than on other types of road. The length of the warning will be determined by circumstances, but in any case should consist of only one flash.

Arm Signal

The arm signal should be given to emphasise an intention or to confirm a mechanical signal already given, more so in bright sunshine when the direction indicators might not be seen due to the brightness of the sun reflecting on the indicators. An arm signal should be used when slowing down on the approach to a pedestrian crossing: in so doing, pedestrians will be aware of your intention to slow down or stop.

One signal many drivers do not use these days is an acknowledgement of a courtesy extended by another road user. All the driver should do to indicate appreciation is raise a hand; it should not be overdone, but nor should it be neglected, because its general use can do much to promote good road manners.

Above left:
Whenever the driver stops to give precedence to a pedestrian, he must not signal the pedestrian to cross the road. When the driver has brought the vehicle to rest, it is up to the pedestrian to decide whether to cross the road or not.

Left:
There are circumstances when pedestrians will not see a signal, because they are blind. The driver should be especially careful on the approach to a junction, and wait until the pedestrian is on the pavement before proceeding further.

6. Road Signs, Observation and Signals

Audible Signals: The Horn

The driver should sound the horn only when it is really necessary: it is a warning of his presence, even though every other precaution has been taken. Its use will at times be necessary to attract the attention of other road users, particularly pedestrians and cyclists who are unaware of an approaching vehicle.

The Advanced Driver's experience and intuition must be the criteria upon which the driver decides whether a horn note is required. In heavy traffic the use of the horn is rare, because speeds are moderate and other actions can be taken in good time. It must be realised that when the horn is used it gives no protection or right of way whatsoever. There have been fatal accidents caused by drivers using the horn and in so doing mistakenly assuming the road ahead will be clear by the time the hazard is reached. The horn warning should be used in good time, not in an aggressive manner or a way that will frighten other road users. The use of the horn must comply with the rules stated in the *Highway Code*.

Above right:
A vehicle can be seen leaving a private driveway — a typical situation where the horn would be used as a warning of your presence, as you can see the driver's vehicle but he cannot see yours.

Right:
A vehicle that was obscured by the bus is trying to emerge despite the limited vision. In this typical situation it would not be necessary to sound the horn, as a reduction of speed and giving the emerging vehicle precedence is all that is required.

Far right:
The children playing at the kerb present a major hazard. A driver approaching this situation should apply the appropriate Features of the System of Car Control, and, if necessary, stop. The use of the horn should be considered with care, as it could frighten the children and increase the danger.

7 Positioning

Positioning

Positioning is of paramount importance before cornering and for road observation. The Advanced Driver will apply Feature One of the System of Car Control — Course — to any hazard, so that the vehicle will be in the correct position on the road at the approach to the hazard. To adopt the correct course he must take into account the position of other traffic and the presence of stationary vehicles, lane markings and any other potential danger, whether visible or not. This will enable the driver to gain the best possible view of the road ahead and to either side, thus increasing his margin of safety in relation to the actual and possible danger ahead and to either side of him.

Left:
The driver has observed the crossroads ahead, and noted the restricted view to either side of the junction. He has implemented Features One and Two of the System, being aware of any following traffic; it is safe to have changed course to just left of the centre of the road in order to gain maximum observation of the junction. Speed has not been reduced.

Below left:
There will be occasions when a driver will have to change course or even stop, due to the position and size of another vehicle. The heavy goods vehicle is travelling on the wrong side of the road due to the presence of a dangerously parked car. It should be borne in mind that the amount of road space required for the heavy goods vehicle to complete the manoeuvre is considerable.

7. Positioning

Right:
The driver is in the right place on the road, travelling at the right speed with the right gear engaged. He is making no effort to overtake the cyclist until the wandering dog and approaching vehicle are cleared; by doing so, he is not adding danger to that which is evident at the time.

Below right:
The driver has applied Feature One (Course), thus being in the safest position on the road for prevailing conditions. The potential dangers can be seen, therefore Feature Two of the System (Mirrors, Signals and Speed) must be considered and used when necessary.

Far right below:
The driver has applied Feature One (Course) close to the nearside, to allow the approaching bus to pass a stationary vehicle. In so doing he must apply Feature Two (Mirrors, Signals and Speed), as it will be necessary to reduce speed to that required to pass the market area with safety. He must look in the mirrors and consider the need for a slowing down signal, bearing in mind that he may have to apply his brakes. Therefore other road users in front and behind should be informed of his intention to slow down and stop. He should aim to lose all unwanted road speed by deceleration, if the circumstances allow.

Left:
There are numerous examples why a driver will have to change course from that of a normal driving position. The road markings on the left represent the line of the kerb, thus allowing drivers emerging from the driveways a clear view to their right before emerging on to the road. The driver should comply with the road markings and position his vehicle as shown.

Far left below:
The traffic signs warn the driver of potential danger. Therefore the decision to reduce speed and select a course that will give him the greatest possible margin of safety should be taken, bearing in mind the driver is approaching a left hand bend that has a restricted view of the road ahead.

Below left:
It will be explained that on the approach to a left hand bend, advantage can often be gained by positioning the vehicle close to the centre line, with the purpose of obtaining an earlier view. But common sense must prevail on the approach to any hazard: the approaching heavy goods vehicle, fully laden and suspension working hard, is travelling at a speed far in excess of the bounds of safety, and is partially over the double white lines. This is typical of situations that occur, and therefore the course must be selected carefully, otherwise a serious or fatal accident could result.

7. Positioning

Right:

When being overtaken, a driver should, if the situation demands and it is practically possible, adopt a position well to the left and consider reducing speed, allowing the driver that is overtaking time to return to the left, and out of danger.

If the overtaking car and the approaching heavy goods vehicle shown are travelling at 60mph, the closing speed would be 176ft/sec. Misjudgement of speed and distance is the cause of many fatal accidents.

Below right:

A good driver is always in the correct position on the road, not only when an obvious hazard is seen, but at all times. One of the dangers a driver must consider before applying Feature One (Course) is that of approaching traffic, as shown here. The approaching vehicle is well over the centre lines, giving the cyclist a good margin of safety while overtaking, but has ignored the possibility of approaching traffic. This typical situation must be borne in mind at the approach to all bends.

Far right:

The advance warning sign and road markings inform the driver of potential danger. Each Feature of the System of Car Control must be considered and used as necessary, thereby adopting a safe approach to the hazard, also bearing in mind the situation could change at any moment.

Far left:
Ice, slush and snow make the cyclist's journey a precarious one. The driver should bear in mind that the cyclist could come off his bicycle at any moment, therefore a good safety position must be maintained and the normal stopping distance at least trebled. Any attempt to overtake the cyclist should be delayed until the road ahead can be seen to be clear.

Above left:
The driver is approaching an off-set crossroads with the intention of going to North Tawton. When applying the System of Car Control in this situation, no signal is necessary because it could mislead other road users of the true intention.

Left:
The driver, who is in the presence of potential danger on all sides, will have applied each Feature of the System as necessary, to ensure that the vehicle will be in the right place on the road, travelling at the right speed, and with the right gear engaged. If parking is considered, the information given by the traffic sign must be borne in mind.

7. Positioning

Right:
When pedestrian traffic is heavy, the driver should never take it for granted that pedestrians will apply the 'Green Cross Code' before stepping off the footpath. The majority of pedestrians seen here are crossing the road in a carefree manner, and by doing so create danger to themselves and other road users. For this reason the driver should adopt a position nearer the crown of the road, so that a better view is obtained.

Above left:
When travelling on a primary route, some drivers pull in a lay-by for a rest or refreshment. The driver approaching a lay-by should, if possible, position the vehicle close to the white line, thus allowing an extra margin of safety for mistakes made by drivers leaving the lay-by. The observant driver will look for clues, like the position of the front wheels of the heavy goods vehicle and a puff of exhaust smoke when the engine is started.

Left:
An obvious clue was given in the previous picture as to what could happen. The heavy goods vehicle now leaves the lay-by; it has only taken a few seconds for a given situation to change, and passing traffic can be involved.

7. Positioning

Right:
When catching up with another vehicle that is straddling two lanes on a dual carriageway, the driver should consider sounding the horn and wait until the vehicle in front decides on its course of action. It must be borne in mind that there are junctions on either side of the vehicle in front, therefore the decision to overtake cannot be made until the junctions have been passed, thus complying with the *Highway Code.*

Below right:
This vehicle has broken down on a roundabout, obstructing the lane that was to be used. The observant driver will have looked across the roundabout to see the potential danger in good time. He must use the mirrors, give a deviation signal if required, and, having regard to the volume and position of any other traffic, adopt a course to go round the hazard. Other Features of the System should be used as and when necessary.

Far right:
In a road where vehicles have parked opposite each other, the driver confronted with an approaching vehicle has no option but to give way and position the vehicle ready to proceed when the way is clear, thereby allowing the approaching vehicle a clear passage.

Left:

Width restrictions control the use of some roads in towns. The driver approaching such a restriction should look in the mirrors and then apply Feature One (Course). Applying Feature Two (Mirrors, Signals and Speed), the mirrors should be used again, and, if needed, a further reduction of speed should be made; no signal is required unless a change of direction is intended after the restriction. For Feature Three (Gear), the gear selected should be appropriate to the road speed of the vehicle. When the hazard has been passed, the mirrors (Feature Four) should be used to check the movement of any following traffic, and use of the horn (Feature Five) considered. Finally, applying Feature Six (Acceleration), the correct degree of acceleration should be employed to leave the hazard safely.

Left:

The driver approaching a road on the nearside should look into it as early as practically possible. The driver on the left, waiting to emerge, can be seen looking for approaching traffic. However, this is not always the case, and the driver should approach this type of junction with caution, getting the greatest possible margin of safety by positioning the vehicle close to the centreline. If eye contact is not made with the driver on the nearside, the horn (Feature Five) should be sounded so that he is aware of your presence.

7. Positioning

One-Way Systems

When passing a row of stationary vehicles, there is always a possibility of pedestrians stepping out between them. Where such dangers exist it is safer to adopt a position nearer the crown of the road, to obtain a better view. This will give the driver more space in which to take avoiding action, should it become necessary.

Above right:

The driver passing a row of stationary vehicles on the left or right side should look for potential danger: eg, a car door opening or a pedestrian stepping off the pavement. A safe road position must be maintained. Here the pedestrian has stepped off the pavement and is looking for approaching traffic. Not all pedestrians are as careful as this one.

Far right above:

Some one-way systems have a central refuge like the one shown. The road markings, combined with the traffic sign, give a clear message.

Right:

At the end of most one-way systems there are usually traffic lanes. The driver should be in the correct lane for the direction in which he intends to travel.

Single Track Roads

When travelling along a single track road a driver should make due allowance for the possibility that another vehicle may appear around the next bend. It must be understood that the combined speeds of two opposing vehicles will reduce the distance available for stopping, subject to the drivers having an average reaction time of 0.7 seconds.

Far left:
Because of the width of the road, vehicles can only move in one direction at a time; when an approaching vehicle can be seen the driver should pull into the special passing place and allow the approaching vehicle to pass. If the passing place is on the other side of the road, the driver should wait opposite it and let the approaching vehicle use the passing place.

The places provided for passing should be kept clear for passing: a driver must not park the vehicle in a passing place.

Above left:
When following an agricultural vehicle on a single track road, the driver has no option but to 'follow my leader' and maintain a safe following distance, which will assist his zone of vision. It must be borne in mind that the direction indicator and stop light signals could be inoperable, and any arm signal given by the driver obscured by the trailer.

Left:
On some roads it is impractical to have road markings along the carriageway. In this example the road is not wide enough for two opposing vehicles to pass if they are travelling at excessive speed, even though they may be complying with the law for the type of road. The driver should never assume that the approaching vehicle will give him right of way: if that assumption is made and it is wrong, a serious accident could occur.

7. Positioning

8 Cornering

The manner in which some drivers attack corners and bends can only be classed as suicidal. They drive regardless of the conditions prevailing, and for them the why and wherefore of a safe driving plan does not exist in any form. Only fate determines the future of such drivers in a given situation.

The various types of corners and bends approached in day-to-day motoring must be negotiated with complete safety. This can only be achieved if a thorough understanding of vehicle control is mastered.

Cornering is such an important feature of driving that it is essential that the driver has a thorough understanding of its theory and principles of safety.

ROAD CAMBER OR CROSS FALL

When cornering, the System of Car Control can only be implemented correctly if the driver applies the principles and safety factors of cornering in good time.

Right:
A right hand bend which has an adverse camber is unfavourable, because the vehicle will tend to slide down the slope, particularly when the road surface is smooth or wet. It must be borne in mind that any reduction of speed by using the brakes should be made on the approach, as braking on a bend is potentially dangerous.

Far right:
This driver approached the bend too fast, braked hard on the bend and lost control of the vehicle. Notice how the rear of the car is sliding down the camber, in all probability into a tree.

The Principles of Cornering

(1) Having recognised the bend, make proper use of the mirrors to check the movement of following traffic, and check the road well ahead for approaching traffic. If safe to do so, move to the correct position on the road so that maximum visibility is gained on the approach. It must be borne in mind that no inconvenience or potential danger must arise from the vehicle's course.

(2) When on course, check the speed of the vehicle — is it excessive or too slow for the situation? — and adjust accordingly.

3) Select the correct gear for the speed required.
4) Subject to the conditions prevailing, the speed of the vehicle should be maintained constant while negotiating the bend.

Safety Factors

If the principles are applied at all times, then the driver will have the vehicle under control on the approach to, during and leaving the bend or corner: combined with compliance with the *Highway Code* they leave nothing to chance. Remember:

1) The vehicle should be in the correct position on the road, unless circumstances dictate otherwise.
2) The correct speed on the approach will enable the vehicle to remain so on the exit.
3) As at any other time, the driver must be able to stop the vehicle within the distance that can be seen to be clear.

A System of Car Control for Bends

In order to apply the principles of Car Control correctly, it is of the utmost importance that a driver should recognise the different types of bend. This can only be achieved by good powers of observation. Under the heading 'Road Observation' it has been mentioned that a driver with good powers of observation will recognise potential danger well ahead. This applies to any type of hazard, and merely to observe the road disappearing round a bend is insufficient.

It must be stressed that brief but valuable views of the road ahead can only be achieved by looking through gaps in hedgerows, buildings or trees. Furthermore, trees, hedgerows, lamp standards and telegraph poles lining the verge ahead will give some indication of the severity of the bend: therefore an early assessment can be made, and speed and position adjusted accordingly.

Feature One: Course (see page 102)

The driver, having seen the hazard, decides on the correct line of approach. He looks in the mirrors and is therefore aware of any following traffic, and positions the vehicle close to the nearside, thereby maintaining the best view. Consideration must be given to dangers that cannot be seen — ie, a concealed entrance or junction — plus the condition of the road surface, camber and weather conditions at the time.

Feature Two: Mirrors, Signals and Speed

If the speed has to be reduced for the bend, the mirrors should be used before slowing down; a signal at this point is not normally required, but should be considered. The factors that determine the correct speed of approach are:

● What can and cannot be seen of the road ahead.
● The severity of the bend and the width of the road available.
● The condition of the road surface.
● The position and/or the possible presence of other road users.
● The road-holding qualities of the vehicle and the driver's ability to cope with the speed whilst following the contours of the road.

Feature Three: Gear

If speed has been reduced, the correct gear must be selected to drive round the bend at a constant speed with the engine just pulling. If the gear has not been changed and the speed allows, it should respond readily to use of the accelerator.

Feature Four: Mirrors and Signals

The driver should then check the mirrors, so that he will be fully aware of any following traffic, before entering the hazard. Again, a signal at this point is not normally required, but should be considered.

Feature Five: Horn

When the view of the road is seen to be clear, an audible warning would be of no use. When approaching blind bends where safety margins are limited, the horn should be used as a warning of the driver's presence.

Feature Six: Acceleration

The bend should be negotiated at a constant speed, with the engine just pulling, therefore the gear should be such as to meet these requirements. There will be circumstances where this will not apply and where deceleration and even braking may be necessary: for example:

● When descending a hill.
● When the presence of traffic ahead makes it unsafe, thus illogical.
● On dangerous road surfaces, such as ice, snow, mud and oil.

These factors must be borne in mind, as well as the contours of the road and the rate at which a clear view ahead can be seen. This latter point will vary, from just past the apex to where the road straightens, as can be seen in the following photographs.

Right:

At this point the driver maintains his present course, close to the nearside of the road. He should then look in the mirrors to check the movement of any following traffic. As the road ahead can be seen to be clear, he can then select a course towards the centre of the road.

Far right:

The driver has positioned his vehicle just left of the centre line, following the most shallow curve and thus reducing the radial force to the nearside, thereby improving the stability of the vehicle.

Below right:

Constant observation of the road ahead and across the bend is of paramount importance. Tram-lining round a bend (keeping well to the left on the arc of a left hand bend) at speed will increase the radial force on the car, impairing its stability.

This driver is approaching a left hand bend, and his vision ahead is adequate for the speed at which the vehicle is travelling.

Far right:

This position to the left of the centre line is maintained until the view of the road opens up. At this point the vehicle is driven through a gradual curved path towards the nearside of the road, thus achieving the same advantages of observation as for the course for entering a right hand bend.

Driving Through a Series of Bends

Right:
The driver has eased the vehicle back to the nearside, thereby being in the correct position (Course) to maintain the best view. At this stage, each Feature of the System should be considered. If speed has been constant throughout the bends, due to good visibility of the road ahead and absence of other road users, there should be no need to change gear.

Far right:
The driver, approaching the last of a series of bends that bears to the right, can see a traffic sign ahead warning him of the danger of a crossroads. A gap in the hedge indicates the location of the junction. At this stage the driver should use his mirrors and plan his course for the hazard.

Right:
As the driver leaves the last curve and the road straightens up, any increase in speed will be governed by the state of the road surface, vision and the presence of traffic. In no circumstances must any road user be endangered or inconvenienced while negotiating a curve; to achieve this end the System of Car Control is strictly adhered to. The driver, concentrating on the hazard ahead, looks in the mirrors: if safe to do so, he selects the course that will give the maximum margin of safety.

Far right:
The driver has selected a safe position on the road, as described in 'Positioning'.

Above right:

There will be occasions when it is impossible to obtain any advance information, such as the example of tall hedges shown. The severity of the bend *can* be assessed on the approach, by noting the way the offside and nearside verges meet on the same axis; thus if the verges continue to meet as the driver enters the bend, it is obvious the severity of the bend is sharp. The position of the vehicle on the approach to a sharp left hand bend should be close to the centre line, with the object of gaining an earlier view.

Right:

It is not until the apex of the bend is reached that parked vehicles and an approaching vehicle can be seen.

Above left:
POSITIONING THE VEHICLE FOR A BETTER VIEW OF A LEFT HAND BEND
By positioning the vehicle well to the nearside, a driver's view of the road ahead would be very limited, due to the severity of the bend, the width of the road and thick hedges. By implementing each required Feature of the System in good time, his road position will increase his view of the road ahead.

Left:
By changing road position, approaching traffic can be seen in good time. No other road user or pedestrian should be endangered or inconvenienced at any time by the action of the driver, for any reason or circumstance.

8. Cornering

Above right:
COURSE SELECTED FOR A SHARP RIGHT HAND BEND
The System applied, the driver has adopted the correct position (Course) to obtain the best view. The use of the horn is advised, because of the sharp bend and the restricted margin of safety.

Right:
There are many situations, as explained in the *Highway Code*, where overtaking is forbidden. It only takes one careless driver, overtaking on the approach to a sharp bend, and oblivious of any danger, to cause a lot of damage and injury to other road users. In this, and similar situations, the defensive driver should be aware of and take appropriate action, so as not to get involved. Note that the example illustrated was *not* a posed one.

9 Overtaking

Overtaking

Thoughtless overtaking at the wrong time and place has been the cause of many fatal road accidents. During his journey, a driver will pass many stationary and moving vehicles; those travelling in the same direction as himself he is said to 'overtake'. To do so safely, the System of Car Control must be applied: although the System is the same as that for fixed hazards, it is more complex, because during the process of overtaking, a number of subsidiary hazards may arise and have to be dealt with in conjunction with the primary hazard.

Passing a stationary vehicle on the nearside of the road requires some thought, but presents little difficulty. The mirrors must be used well before applying Feature One (Course), and moving out to pass the obstruction. The driver must consider using each Feature of the System in sequence and as necessary. The horn (Feature Five) may need to be sounded if the stationary vehicle is occupied or there are signs of activity in or around it. On other occasions, where approaching traffic makes it unsafe to pass (see 'Positioning'), the driver must vary his speed and gear or even stop altogether. A slow moving vehicle (eg, a heavy goods vehicle going uphill) could increase its speed, making planning more difficult and judgement more critical.

Far left:
The most dangerous road carrying two-way traffic is the one marked with three lanes, the overtaking lane each way being the central lane. A driver approaching the above situation should be aware of the potential danger of approaching vehicles encroaching on his lane. He should also be fully aware of any following vehicles.

Left:
When a driver realises that he is catching up with another vehicle (closing gap), he must make up his mind either to adjust his speed and follow it, or overtake at the first opportunity. Here the driver can see an approaching vehicle and therefore reduces speed until he can see the road to be clear. He can then decide whether to overtake or hold back.

9. Overtaking

Right:
The driver has reduced speed, waiting for the approaching vehicle in the middle lane to pass: then the decision can be made to overtake. In so doing, he creates no danger and will not become 'the meat in the sandwich'.

Below right:
This driver is catching up a slower-moving vehicle in the absence of approaching vehicles or other hazards. The driver need only check the mirrors, and if safe to do so, he can move out to a course (Feature One) to pass the vehicle with plenty of room. When the vehicle that has been overtaken can be seen in the mirrors (flat glass type), the driver should move back to the nearside.

In this type of situation it may not be necessary to change speed or gear from the time when the vehicle is first seen to when it is overtaken. Experience plays a great part in judgements, and the decision to overtake must include an assessment of the speed of vehicle(s) concerned and distance involved, such as:

● The speed of vehicle(s) to be overtaken.
● The speed and performance of the driver's own vehicle.
● The speed of any approaching vehicle(s) that could come into or is in view.
● The distance that is going to be covered while overtaking.

Reversing

During a driver's career, the need to turn his vehicle round to face the opposite direction arises on many occasions. One of the most difficult and potentially dangerous manoeuvres is that of reversing a vehicle round a corner, more so when pedestrians are present on the footpath. For this reason the driver should select a suitable corner where danger and inconvenience to pedestrians and other road users is at a minimum.

During the hours of darkness and in poor daylight visibility, a vehicle that has no reversing lights fitted to illuminate the area of road to the rear of the vehicle, can be potentially dangerous. A driver can assist the situation by using the brake lights or the light of a directional indicator to gain a better view, taking care not to mislead other road users when the ancillary light is in use.

A driver who has to reverse a commercial vehicle round a corner should bear in mind the large area to the rear of the vehicle that is blind to him, and should obtain assistance from a reliable person.

Above left:
The driver has found a suitable corner to reverse round, the area having been scanned for obstructions. All the car windows are clear and therefore an unobstructed view is available.

When safe to move off, the driver should travel slowly, slipping the clutch as necessary. In a vehicle that has an automatic gearbox, the speed of the vehicle may be checked by use of the left foot on the brake.

Left:
On reaching the corner, the driver should take all-round observation for potential danger. He must bear in mind that when the steering is turned left, the front of the vehicle will move out, thus striking nearby unnoticed objects.

9. Overtaking

Above right:
The speed of the vehicle should be that of a slow walking man at all times — ie, under control and with due regard for other road users.

Right:
The seat belt has been undone to allow freedom of movement. One hand is placed at the top of the steering wheel, and the other hand may adopt a low position. The method of turning the steering wheel is that used for normal driving, unless, of course, a driver has a physical disability.

Far right:
When the driver has reversed into the side road and is clear of the junction, he should then carry out the procedure for moving off and apply each feature of the System as appropriate.

The Turn in the Road

The alternative to reversing round a corner is to turn the vehicle round in the road. The majority of qualified drivers today are aware of these manoeuvres, having carried them out as part of their basic driving test to obtain a group A or B driving licence.

The driver should find a side road that is suitable for this manoeuvre, and carry out the following movements. Throughout this manoeuvre, the driver should travel slowly, slipping the clutch as necessary.

Also it is possible, particularly in a vehicle fitted with power assisted steering, for sufficient effort to be exerted on the steering wheel to move the road wheels when the vehicle is stationary. This practice should be avoided because of the strain imposed on the steering linkage. The steering wheel should not be moved unless the vehicle is moving.

One of the main reasons why some 28% of drivers fail the Advanced Driving Test is lack of judgement and control whilst manoeuvring and reversing.

Left:
A suitable position has been found and the driver is ready to move off. He checks his mirrors and looks round to get unobscured observation. When the road is clear, the hand brake is released; the vehicle should be moved slowly and smoothly and at the same time the steering wheel should be turned quickly to the right.

Far left:
The driver has applied full right lock and is looking to his offside. When the front offside wheel is about 4ft from the kerb the steering wheel should be turned quickly to the left.

Left:
The driver has applied full left lock and stopped the vehicle with the front offside wheel close to the kerb. Next he has applied the hand brake and selected reverse gear. He then looks right, left and right again.

Far left:
Satisfied it is safe to move off, the driver releases the hand brake and moves the vehicle slowly back. He is looking over his left shoulder as he turns the steering wheel quickly to the left.

Left:
The left lock applied, the driver now looks to his offside and turns the steering wheel quickly to the right.

9. Overtaking

Right:
The driver takes into account the overhang of the rear of his vehicle, thus stopping the vehicle when the rear is about 2ft from the kerb.

Far right:
With the hand brake applied and first gear selected, the driver looks right, left and right again. When he is sure it is safe to move off, the hand brake is released and the vehicle is moved slowly and smoothly forward.

Below right:
With a full right steering lock applied, the vehicle is moving slowly and smoothly under full control.

Far right below:
Just before the vehicle runs parallel with the kerb, the steering is turned quickly to the left. When the vehicle is level with the kerb, the mirrors are checked: if safe to do so, normal driving may be resumed.

Left:
The driver, seeing a suitable parking place that is at least 1½ times the length of the vehicle being driven, must use the mirrors and if necessary give an arm signal of the intention to slow down and stop.

Far left below:
The vehicle should be brought to rest at least one metre from the vehicle on the nearside. The driver should then get ready to reverse the vehicle into the space seen.

Below left:
The driver must scan all around for potential danger before the manoeuvre can be started; if in any doubt, wait to make sure it is safe to proceed.

Parking the Vehicle Parallel with the Kerb

Finding a safe place to park and complying with the law in busy cities is an ever-increasing and often frustrating problem. For the uninitiated the following safety procedures should be adopted and used if parallel parking is to be achieved at the first attempt.

9. Overtaking

Right:
When the driver is sure it is safe to proceed, the vehicle should be moved slowly with the clutch partially engaged, thus allowing the vehicle to be moved at a crawling speed. The driver should look to the front before the steering wheel is turned to the left, as the front of the vehicle will swing out, thus causing potential danger, as can be seen.

Right:
At this stage of the manoeuvre the driver should still be looking over his left shoulder. The steering wheel should now be turned quickly to the right.

Far right:
The rear of the vehicle is approaching the kerb at the correct angle, with a right steering lock being applied. The vehicle is moving at a crawling pace. As the front nearside of the vehicle moves towards the kerb, the driver should at this stage check the front for adequate safety clearance between the two vehicles, otherwise the nearside front of the vehicle could collide with the rear offside of the parked vehicle.

Right:
When the vehicle is parallel with the kerb, the steering wheels will in all probability still have a right lock on. The driver should move the vehicle slowly forward, at the same time turning the steering wheel quickly to the left, so that the steering wheels are parallel with the car and kerb.

Below right:
With the vehicle and steering wheels parallel with the kerb, the driver should generally have to move the vehicle forward or backward so that an equal space is made between the car in front and the one behind, thus allowing any of the three vehicles to get out. However, as illustrated here, due consideration must be given to where the driver can and cannot park; for example, blocking a vehicle entrance to properties. The driver must comply with the waiting and parking restrictions listed in the *Highway Code*.

Far right:
When the driver has completed the manoeuvre, the vehicle should be parallel with the kerb and should not protrude beyond other vehicles unnecessarily. The procedure for stopping and leaving the vehicle should be implemented.

9. Overtaking

Right:
The driver, seeing a suitable parking place, must use the mirrors and, if necessary, give an arm signal to slow down and stop. The vehicle should be brought to rest at least one metre from the vehicle on the nearside. The driver should then get ready to reverse the vehicle into the space seen. All-round observation should be taken for potential danger before the manoeuvre can be started; if in any doubt, the driver should wait to make sure it is safe to proceed.

Right:
When the driver is sure it is safe to proceed, the vehicle should be moved slowly with the clutch partially engaged, thus allowing the vehicle to be moved at a crawling speed. The driver should look to the front and to either side before the steering wheel is turned to the left, as the front of the vehicle will swing out, thus causing potential danger.

Far right:
The driver is applying full left steering lock, while looking over his left shoulder.

Parking in a Car Park

Similar to parallel parking is parking in a car park, where parking spaces generally are marked out. It is important that the vehicle is in the middle of the marked space when the manoeuvre is completed, unless circumstances dictate otherwise.

Above right:
With left steering lock applied, the rear of the vehicle is approaching the parking space at the correct angle.

Right:
At this stage, the driver should check for adequate safety clearance.

Far right:
When the manoeuvre is completed, the vehicle should be parallel with the markings of the parking space, and equal distance from the vehicles on either side. The procedure for stopping and leaving the vehicle should be implemented.

EXAMPLES OF DANGEROUS AND INCONSIDERATE PARKING

Right:
A driver's view of the Pelican Crossing is obscured by the two vehicles parked on the right, thus creating a potentially dangerous situation for pedestrians and traffic.

Far right:
It is an offence to park or wait on the zig-zag areas of a pedestrian crossing, therefore the driver of the van with the tail gate open is breaking the law.

Below right:
Having completed a delivery at a building site, the driver has moved his vehicle on to the road and left it opposite a continuous white line, thereby committing an offence.

Far right below:
This inconsiderate and illegal parking has created a potentially dangerous situation for drivers trying to emerge into the junction. A driver's view to his left is obstructed by vehicles parked too close to the junction.

Stopping and Leaving the Vehicle

A driver who intends to park his vehicle on the public highway should implement Feature Two of the System. The mirrors should be used to check the movements and position of following traffic, bearing in mind that it will be necessary to apply the brakes. A signal by direction indicator or arm should be considered to inform other road users and pedestrians of the intention to deviate or slow down. Speed should be reduced gradually, having due regard to traffic that can be following too closely.

The driver should bring his vehicle to rest in a safe position close to the kerb. It cannot be emphasised enough that the driver must comply with the *Highway Code* whenever he parks his vehicle — except in circumstances beyond his control or to avoid an accident — otherwise he will be breaking the law.

When the driver has brought his vehicle to rest, his foot should remain on the brake pedal until the hand brake is applied and neutral selected. If the vehicle is on a gradient, first gear should be selected if the vehicle is facing uphill, and reverse gear selected for that of a down hill gradient, as an additional safety precaution. The engine and all unnecessary auxiliaries should then be switched off, and the seat belt stored neatly. For a vehicle with an automatic gearbox, the gear selector should be moved to the 'P' position.

The driver should make sure it is safe to get out of the vehicle. He should look in his mirrors and over his shoulder for passing traffic, and only when it is safe to do so, should he open the door. Likewise, a passenger should look over his shoulder to make sure it is safe to open the door, otherwise a pedestrian could be injured.

Before leaving the vehicle unattended, the driver should carry out the following checks:

- Remove the ignition key and activate the steering lock.
- Close all windows.
- Put any valuables out of sight, preferably in the boot.
- Lock all doors, the boot and sun roof.

Far left:
The Wheel Clamp, the deterrent to illegal, dangerous and inconsiderate motorists.

Left:
The experienced driver remembers the old proverb 'Lock it or lose it'. Like this driver, make sure you lock your doors.

9. Overtaking

10 Motorways and Dual Carriageways

Motorways have been designed and constructed to provide safer travelling, reduce the time taken to make a journey, and to carry more traffic. This objective has been achieved, making a significant contribution to the national economy and being a benefit to the community.

For a variety of reasons, new parliamentary powers were needed to construct the new special roads. In 1949 the royal assent was given to the Special Roads Act of 1949, which made possible the building of roads such as motorways for the exclusive use of certain types of motor traffic. Those types not included are banned from motorways completely. The Act also gave the necessary powers to alter or close any side road, public footpath or private driveway which crosses the route of the special road.

The first motorway constructed in the United Kingdom was the Preston by-pass officially opened on 5 December 1958 by the Prime Minister, Mr Harold Macmillan. It was eight miles long and is now part of the M6. The next motorway to be constructed was the London-Yorkshire M1. Mr Ernest Marples opened the 72 miles of motorway between Aldenham and Crick on 11 April 1960.

When designing a motorway, surveyors and engineers have to include many safety factors. The average driver is not aware of these, which appear to be taken for granted.

Standards of Alignment

On some motorways there are curves but no bends. Due to the higher speed that traffic travels on motorways, compared with other types of road, it is essential that a driver has a good view of the road ahead. It should be understood that 'sight distance' is the clear distance over which a driver, entering a curve, is able to see an obstruction from an assumed eye level of 3ft 6in above the surface of the road. The minimum sight distance required along rural motorways is 295m (950ft), in both vertical and horizontal planes. This sight distance is equivalent to the minimum stopping distance for a speed of 70mph while travelling round a curve, if there was an obstruction ahead. A vehicle travelling at 70mph would cover a distance of 950ft in nine seconds.

Considering the preliminary alignment of the route, the design layout of a motorway supplied by the surveyor has to incorporate the significance of sight distance in relation to the curvature, bridges and other fixtures that could obstruct a driver's view, with economics in mind. An urban motorway was defined, at the 1956 London Conference on Motorways, as a motorway running through a built-up area, and a rural one as a motorway which does not. The only other difference is that on an urban motorway the central reservation is narrower, and the hard shoulder is 2m wide compared with 3.3m wide on a rural motorway.

It must be borne in mind that smooth and hard wearing road surfaces are provided on motorways, but these may have a very low coefficient of friction when wet. In adverse weather conditions, the stopping distance should be at least trebled.

After travelling some distance on a motorway, there is a tendency for a driver to increase speed without being aware of the fact. Long straight stretches can have a hypnotic and monotonous effect and can affect a driver by what is called Parallelism, especially when the driver is tired. This is why motorways have curves, to prevent Parallelism and help the driver remain alert.

Joining and Leaving a Motorway

Drivers join a motorway from a slip road that progresses into an acceleration lane. The majority of slip lanes have a downhill gradient, thereby assisting the driver to increase his road speed to that of traffic on the motorway. Most acceleration lanes are parallel to the main carriageway and are about 800ft in length.

A driver must give way to traffic on the carriageway. If he forces his way into the traffic on the motorway, he is committing an offence, and in so doing is causing drivers to brake or change course to avoid a collision. If a signal is used when joining a motorway, it gives no right of way whatsoever.

Left:
The driver should use the downhill gradient to adjust to an appropriate road speed, then join the motorway when safe to do so.

Below:
When intending to leave the motorway, the driver must position the vehicle in the left hand lane in good time. If applicable, a signal should be given. The deceleration lane is approximately 500ft long, and it is on it where the majority of braking is done, not on the carriageway. The slip lane has an uphill gradient to assist the driver to reduce speed.

There are some slip lanes, however, that have a downhill gradient; therefore speed must be reduced in good time.

10. Motorways and Dual Carriageways

Right:
The sign informs the driver that he is at the start of the motorway and must therefore comply with the rules stated in the *Highway Code*.

Far right:
The sign informs the driver that he is at the end of the motorway. At this stage the driver should have applied each Feature of the System as necessary.
After travelling at fairly fast speeds, the sensation of travelling slower when speed is brought down to leave the motorway will make it seem as if the vehicle is crawling along. In this circumstance the driver is advised to look at the speedometer to confirm the true speed of the vehicle.

Below right:
Some slip roads have sharp bends, therefore speed must be reduced on the straight part of the slip road, before arriving at the bend.

Left:

On some slip roads, yellow speed hatch markings are provided to assist drivers, but some drivers do not take heed of the warning given. The space between the lines is decreased as the hazard is approached. Combined with the additional thickness compared with white lane markings, they warn drivers who are driving too fast to reduce speed.

Below left:

Regardless of the warning given by the yellow hatch markings, it is evident that there are many drivers who reduce speed too late, as the tyre marks prove.

Right:

FEATURES OF MOTORWAY CONSTRUCTION

Where there is considerable traffic movement at an interchange, or the interchange is complex, overhead gantry signs are used to direct traffic into the correct lane, well in advance of the interchange. On rural motorways, the hard shoulder is 3.3m wide, on urban motorways 2m wide. The hard shoulder is of a contrasting texture and colour, and the nearside edge of the carriageway is defined by an edge line of reflectorised white paint (Ballotini). Red reflecting road studs (cat's-eyes) are placed on the nearside of the carriageway.

Reflectorised white paint is used for lane markings. These are 2m in length and 100mm wide, with a 7m gap between each marking. A white cat's-eye is placed at 18m intervals between every other gap in the lines; in areas subject to fog and mist, a cat's-eye is placed in every gap. Amber studs are placed at the edge of the offside lane and central reserve, while green cat's-eyes are placed at the entrances to and exits from slip roads. A double-headed arrow in reflectorised white paint on the carriageway, assists the driver in his intended direction of travel.

The signs, cat's-eyes and road markings are provided to help drivers at night and in poor weather conditions. For them to be of use, it is of the utmost importance that their meaning is understood.

Emergency Telephones

Far left:

Emergency telephones are provided at 1½km intervals on both sides of the motorway, and they are sited in the verge at the back of the hard shoulder. They are orange in colour, and are identified by a number and letter and SOS. Drivers who use the telephones will be in direct contact with the police, whose responsibility it is to answer all emergency calls.

Many thousands of calls are received each year, dealing with breakdowns and kindred matters. Very few calls are concerned directly with police matters, and the remainder are initiated by either negligence or ignorance on the part of motorists, which puts an unnecessary burden on the information room.

Left:

The predominantly white marker posts with a red reflectorised strip are erected on the verge at 100m intervals. The road faces of the posts are marked with a symbol of a telephone and an arrow showing the direction of the nearest emergency telephone.

10. Motorways and Dual Carriageways

Right:
The safety barrier on the central reservation is constructed of corrugated sheet steel, and open box type guard rails are provided at the approach to bridges, and at any point of potential danger. This driver lost control of the vehicle and in consequence crashed into the barrier, which prevented the car from going over the central reservation and causing a more serious accident.

TOLLS

Right:
There are fewer and cheaper tolls in the United Kingdom compared with some European countries. The tolls occur at certain bridges and tunnels.

Far right:
This toll is at Dartford Tunnel on the M25. The driver can either put the correct fee into a hopper, or pay the toll at one of the manned booths. The first service area to be opened on the M25 was at North Mimms.

Road Works

However well a motorway has been constructed, there will come a time when resurfacing or major repairs will be required. As motorways were constructed in lengthy sections, it follows that repairs could extended for several miles with consequent traffic restrictions. This must be borne in mind by the driver who intends to use the motorway while repairs are being carried out.

Road works must be planned carefully, not only to minimise the risk of accidents to the workmen and to users of the motorway, but also to complete the work in the shortest possible time. As a last resort, one side of the carriageway will have to be closed. In such an event, traffic from one side of the motorway will be diverted through the gap in the central reservation to the opposite side of the carriageway; this is called 'contra-flow'. Every precaution should be taken when travelling in what has become a two-way traffic system.

Above left:
The sign warns the driver of road works ahead. The mirrors must be used and Features One and Two of the System considered.

Far left:
The sign informs the driver that a change in course will have to be made. The mirrors must be used to check the movements of following traffic, then Feature One must be applied and Feature Two considered.

Left:
Because of road works, traffic has been diverted through the gap in the central reservation to the opposite side of the carriageway, converting it into a two-way road. The advisory speed limit must be complied with. As can be seen, the hard shoulder is being used as a carriageway.

10. Motorways and Dual Carriageways

Motorway Driving

Right:
This driver, towing a caravan, is following too close to the heavy goods vehicle — the start of what is called 'bunching', the cause of many horrific accidents. When following another vehicle in good weather and road conditions, the two-second rule or a gap of not less than one metre for each mile per hour being travelled should be maintained. This will also leave space for an overtaking vehicle to pull in; when this happens, the mirrors must be used and, if safe to do so, the driver should reduce speed to regain the safe gap.

Right:
A strong crosswind blowing across exposed country is a random factor, like any other weather condition, and must be treated with caution if danger is to be avoided. A crosswind will be most apparent when leaving a sheltered area: ie, passing under a bridge, high embankment or cutting or when being passed by or overtaking a heavy goods vehicle. If the wind is blowing from the left, the driver should apply a little corrective steering lock to the left, and a right corrective lock to combat a strong wind from the right. In strong crosswinds and blustery conditions, the driver should, if safe to do so at the time, reduce speed.

Left:
This type of driver, unaware of the meaning of lane discipline, creates frustration and potential danger to the drivers of the classes of vehicles which are prohibited from using the right-hand lane of a three-lane carriageway. The 'casual users' of motorways, who appear to have little knowledge of the fundamentals of motorway driving or motorway regulations, can be unpredictable in their behaviour. The police endeavour to enforce lane discipline by a verbal warning, but as a last resort will prosecute.

Far left:
Gaps in the central reservation, 17m wide, are provided at intervals of about two miles. They are for emergency use by the police, ambulance and fire services, and for the diversion of traffic from a carriageway when it is blocked, or when repairs are being carried out. No driver is allowed to use the gap unless directed to do so.

Left:
To enable motorway reservation gaps to be easily located in adverse weather, special marker posts with red reflective discs are provided.

10. Motorways and Dual Carriageways

Right:

When operating, overhead gantry signals and matrix markers sited on the verge and central reservation have a double pair of amber lights flashing alternately, and an illuminating symbol giving temporary maximum speeds or information about closed lanes. Flashing red lights indicate STOP.

Far right:

If red lights flash on a slip road, the driver must not pass the sign.

Below right:

The legal powers contained in the Special Roads Act of 1949 restrict motorways to the exclusive use of certain motor traffic. Regulations within the Act govern the use of motorways; every driver should know and understand these before using a motorway. Had drivers done this, the events that have occurred in the past, resulting in chaos and fatal accidents, could in all probability have been avoided.

For numerous reasons, cyclists are banned from motorways, but there is always the one who takes a chance, thereby committing an offence and putting his own, and others', safety in danger.

Temporary maximum speed

Lane(s) closed ahead

End of restriction

Left:
It is an offence to stop on the hard shoulder, other than for reasons of mechanical failure, replacing a punctured tyre, or because of flashing red lights on a traffic signal or when signalled to stop by a police officer. If the driver is allowed in these exceptional circumstances to stop on the hard shoulder or carriageway, the car hazard warning lights (if fitted) should be used.

Crawler Lanes

On motorways, the normal maximum longitudinal gradient in rural areas is 3% (1 in 33). In hilly country a 4% (1 in 25) gradient may exist, when a 1.33 gradient could not reasonably be achieved because of the high cost of deep excavation and other factors involved.

The relative speed differential between classes of vehicles going up a gradient can vary considerably. To minimise the danger of rear end collisions between fast and slow moving vehicles, an additional motorway lane is sometimes provided on the nearside, called a 'Crawler Lane'. There are four times as many accidents on 'A' Class roads compared with motorways, but when accidents do occur on motorways, owing to the speed (or the differential in speeds), they are frequently of the high impact type, and this in many instances accounts for drivers and passengers being trapped in their cabs and cars, with a very high risk of fire.

When horrific concertina crashes occur, it is usually due to vehicles bunching in periods of limited visibility: speed is not reduced on the approach to fog, thus entering the fog at a speed far in excess for the conditions prevailing. It cannot be emphasised enough that Feature Two of the System (Mirrors, Signals and Speed) must be applied on the approach to fog and mist. The average driver does not think there is any danger ahead, until it is seen, then it is too late to take evasive action. In consequence, another pile up has occurred.

Service Areas

On some motorways, 24-hour service areas with adequate parking for private and commercial users are provided. The services available include fuel, a cafeteria or restaurant, and toilet facilities; some service areas have emergency repair facilities and overnight accommodation. Even on these motorways, the driver must check the vehicle fluid levels, tyres (including the spare), tools, fan belt, lights and windscreen wipers/washers, and ensure that the wheels are secure, that all glass is clean, and that all electrical systems are working. In winter, anti-freeze should be added to the cooling system.

It is the responsibility of every driver to ensure that the vehicle he is driving is in a roadworthy condition, and capable of completing the journey. It can be too late when instrument readings and warning lights inform the driver of impending mechanical failure: it can also be very expensive.

10. Motorways and Dual Carriageways

Dual Carriageways

A dual carriageway is similar in some respects to a motorway, but not in others. The national speed limit on a motorway is the same as on the majority of dual carriageways throughout the United Kingdom. However, the legal powers obtained in the Special Roads Act of 1949 restrict motorways to the exclusive use of certain motor traffic, thus allowing a certain specified class of traffic to use it. There are no such restrictions on classes of traffic that can use a dual carriageway.

In the cause of safety, opposing traffic streams are completely separated by a central reserve on both types of road. Collision points are eliminated on motorways by the construction of over or under bridges thus preventing traffic streams crossing each other at the same level. This is not so on dual carriageways.

When driving on a dual carriageway, many drivers travel too fast where hazards exist, because they do not recognise actual or potential danger, believing that the other road user will stop, or that they will be able to stop whatever happens. Speed must be governed by the amount of road that can be and cannot be seen to be clear, and a driver must always be able to stop within the range of his vision by day or by night. An average family saloon travelling at 70mph on a dry road surface will on either type of road take approximately 315ft (22½ car lengths) to stop: adequate distance from the vehicle in front must therefore be maintained at all times.

Top right:
Cyclists are prohibited from using a motorway but can use a dual-carriageway, which has the same speed limit as a motorway. Thus the cyclist shown could turn right at the next intersection, crossing the path of a vehicle travelling at the national speed limit.

Above right:
While in use, this surveyor's vehicle could travel at a speed even less that that of a milk float.

Right:
There have been numerous fatal accidents at intersections; the reasons why they occurred are many. The driver of this tractor, with a trailer in tow, is crossing the dual carriageway: their overall length is such that they block both offside lanes of the dual carriageway. A driver approaching such an intersection should be aware of this type of danger and reduce speed accordingly.

Crossing a Dual Carriageway

Above left:

When crossing a dual carriageway, the driver should treat each half as a separate road. This carriageway has diagonal stripes that extend the width of the central reservation, allowing the driver to wait in the gap in the central dividing strip. However, if the central reservation is too narrow, the driver has no option but to wait in the side road until he can cross the dual carriageway in one movement.

Left:

It is of the utmost importance that the driver positions the vehicle correctly for a right turn, as shown.

10. Motorways and Dual Carriageways

11 General Advice

Breakdowns

In the event of a breakdown or puncture the driver should, if possible, get the vehicle off the road. If for one reason or another this is not possible, any passenger(s) should leave the vehicle and get clear of the road. The driver should then take appropriate action to warn other road users of an obstruction; if the vehicle is fitted with hazard warning lights they should be used. Should a breakdown occur during the hours of darkness, the obligatory (side) lights should be left on together with the hazard warning lights.

In poor daytime visibility and in heavy rain, mist and fog, the same procedure should be carried out as for the hours of darkness. If a red warning sign (a reflecting triangle) is in the vehicle, it should be placed on the road at a reasonable distance from the vehicle for the type of road being used. Should equipment have to be removed from the rear of the vehicle to assist in the repair of the breakdown, every precaution should be taken by the driver, or any one else, not to obscure the rear lamps from approaching traffic, thus defeating their object.

If anything falls from the vehicle being driven, the driver should stop as soon as safely possible. The appropriate hazard lights and side lights should be used, and, when safe to do so, the driver should remove from the carriageway whatever has fallen from the vehicle. This procedure is not allowed on a motorway.

Right:
If the driver has time, the stricken vehicle should be brought to rest on the extreme nearside edge of the road or hard shoulder. If fitted, hazard warning lights should be used, unless the reason for the problem is a breakdown in the electrical system.

Far left, above:
On a motorway, the reflective triangle should be placed on the hard shoulder 150m from the vehicle.

Far left, below:
In this case the reflective triangle should be placed at least 50m from the vehicle.

Left:
Should a breakdown occur just after a bend, it would be useless and irresponsible on the part of the driver to place the triangle 50m from the vehicle. In this situation, the reflective triangle should be placed on the approach to the bend, therefore allowing drivers approaching the obstruction time to act on the information received.

11. General Advice

Driving Through Water

Driving at speed on surface water and in heavy rain can be hazardous, because water-logged tyres will lead to 'aqua planing', more so when the tread depth of the front tyres is near the illegal limit. Aqua planing is a condition when the front tyres cannot cope with undispersed surface water due to the volume of it and the speed of the vehicle, usually in excess of 50mph. When this happens, the tyres push superfluous water forward, creating a wedge; given time and distance, the tyres will mount the wedge and lose contact with the road. The symptoms of aqua planing are light steering; and if speed is maintained, complete loss of steering control will occur. If aqua planing is suspected, deceleration must be immediate, by reducing pressure from the accelerator but not by braking — even momentarily — because this will aggravate the condition. When speed has been reduced considerably the tyres will contact the road surface and steering control will be regained.

Driving at speed into unsuspected deep water — ie, puddles or deep ruts — will in all probability wrench the steering wheel from the hands of the driver, as the wheel reaches the deepest point of the puddle or rut. In consequence, the driver will lose control.

Flood water will collect quickly due to heavy rain or melting snow, especially in poorly drained low lying areas or on uneven road surfaces, at the sides of a cambered road, and where there is a dip under a bridge or underpass.

Many drivers disregard adverse weather conditions and drive too fast for the prevailing conditions. Maintaining an excessive speed in poor visibility caused by spray thrown up by heavy goods vehicles and/or the density of rain, will make flood water difficult to detect on any type of road; this creates potential danger to the driver and other road users.

Right:
If steering control is lost because of driving into deep water too fast, the momentum of a vehicle on a bend is straight ahead, creating danger to an approaching vehicle.

Below right:
This driver, obsessed by speed, has not planned far enough ahead to adopt a course clear of the obvious patch of water, resulting in danger to himself and other road users.

Far right:
A good driver will plan his course well ahead, reduce speed, and, if safe to do so, use the unaffected parts of the road, thereby creating no danger.

Flood Water

Weather conditions can change dramatically, and in a short period of time. It is for this reason that it is not always feasible for warning signs to be placed in areas where danger to the road user is present.

Having seen a warning sign or flood water, the driver should take appropriate action to reduce speed, bearing in mind the position of any other road user, who in all probability has not recognised the danger at the time. The vehicle should be stopped at the edge of the flooded area so that the driver will then have time to assess the situation. The deciding factors whether or not to proceed varies with the type of vehicle being driven. The driver should consider the height of the vehicle, so that no water can enter any part of it (including the exhaust), and be sure that no water will cover the distributor, coil, spark plugs and other electrical components. Furthermore, he should assess the likelihood of hidden obstructions or road subsidence. If the deciding factors are not favourable, there is no alternative but to find another route, thus avoiding the flooded area.

With no alternative to avoiding the flood water, and the deciding factors being favourable, the decision to negotiate the water is made. If the road ahead is clear of any other road user, first gear should be selected and pressure exerted on the accelerator pedal to increase engine speed. The latter is done so that the force of the gases leaving the exhaust pipe prevents the flood water entering or covering the pipe, thus allowing the engine to operate: if water is allowed to cover the opening of the exhaust pipe, the engine will cease to function. When the speed of the engine is selected, the clutch pedal should be released until the tone of the engine changes (this is termed as the 'biting point') and then the clutch and accelerator pedals are held steady. Having checked all round to make sure it is safe to move off, the driver should release the hand brake and move the

Left:
At night, the difference between a wet road surface and flood water is difficult to identify. For some, the consequence has put themselves and others in a dangerous situation.

11. General Advice

vehicle slowly forward, keeping his feet steady. He should proceed through the flood water, controlling the speed of the vehicle by the clutch. (Of course, controlling the speed of the vehicle by slipping the clutch induces wear to the clutch, but as there is no alternative way to control the speed of a vehicle in this situation or some similar ones, the driver has no choice.) Proceed through the flood water maintaining a slow and even speed to avoid making a bow wave; make intelligent use of the shallowest section of the affected parts of the road, bearing in mind at all times the deciding factors — vehicle arrangement and road condition — on which the driver based his decision to proceed.

A driver who has a vehicle with automatic transmission should apply sufficient pressure on the foot brake pedal, then the accelerator as previously explained, and when it is safe to move off the hand brake should be released and the vehicle should move slowly forward. The speed of the vehicle is controlled by the foot brake. Once the driver has passed through the water, he should continue driving slowly and apply the foot brake lightly with the left foot. This last operation needs to be repeated a number of times for short periods, until the driver is satisfied that brake efficiency has been restored fully.

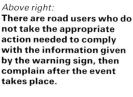

Above right:
There are road users who do not take the appropriate action needed to comply with the information given by the warning sign, then complain after the event takes place.

Right:
The driver of the van has made numerous driving errors, as can be seen by the position of the vehicle, which is about to be abandoned.

Far right:
This sign has reminded the driver to try the brakes: note that the brake lights are on. Test the brakes for their efficiency as soon as reasonably possible.

Above left:
An approaching vehicle will give the driver an idea of the depth of water. However, the information gained must not be taken for granted, as hidden ruts or pot holes can make the water deeper than anticipated.

Left:
This ford has a measure placed to indicate the depth of water, to help drivers determine whether or not to proceed. Always drive slowly through water.

11. General Advice

Broken Windscreens

The common cause of broken windscreens is a stone or other object thrown up from the wheels of another vehicle. It has also been known for a heavy goods vehicle, going up a steep hill with its engine under strain, to create a particular pitch or drone which has shattered a windscreen of a vehicle that is passing. A loud bang is normally associated with a windscreen shattering.

Precautions should be taken by the driver on roads where loose stones or grit are present, by reducing speed and increasing the distance from the vehicle in front. In the event of a windscreen shattering, treat it as an emergency. Generally, it is not advisable to punch a hole in the screen to gain vision, because this may cause injuries and aggravate the situation by allowing pieces of glass to enter the car. All that is necessary is for the driver to pull into the side of the road as soon as practicably possible and to stop.

If it is necessary to continue to drive before the windscreen is replaced, the air vents should be covered and the bodywork protected. The screen should then be pushed outwards and as much glass removed as possible. The vehicle should be driven slowly with the windows closed: this will prevent a through draught and will assist in protecting the driver and passengers from glass splinters. If suitable eye protection is available it should be worn. Sunglasses must not be worn for eye protection during the hours of darkness.

Speed

Ever since the development of the motor vehicle, speed at the wrong time and place has been the cause of many accidents. The choice of speed must be related to the driver's concentration and ability, the type and limitation of the vehicle and the prevailing road and traffic conditions. Remember, that the safe speed for any given situation may change from second to second, therefore speed must be adjusted to suit the situation. Speed is a relative factor and looked upon as something dangerous in itself, but it is dangerous only if used in the wrong place or at the wrong time.

Right:
This is a driver's view of a toughened windscreen the moment it shatters. If travelling at speed it could collapse, creating thousands of fragments of glass which could be blown over the driver and front seat passenger. A laminated windscreen is safer than a toughened screen because it is less likely to shatter.

Far right:
There are statutory speed restrictions in respect of selected areas and classes of vehicles. They have assisted in reducing instances of dangerous high speed driving.

Above left:
The sign warns the driver of the *maximum* speed at which the bend should be approached; even then, a further reduction of speed should be considered as the situation demands.

Left:
The view of the road ahead is obscured because of the bend, and the traffic signs warn the driver of potential danger. The information is received by the driver and each Feature of the System is considered and used in sequence as applicable. He must approach the hazard at a speed such that he can stop within the range of his vision.

11. General Advice

Right:
Driving and road surface conditions were dangerous. This was obvious to many drivers, but not to the driver of the car shown here, who thought the road had been treated with salt. It had not been, and in consequence another accident occurred.

Below right:
Ramps (sleeping policemen) have been placed to deter the driver from driving too fast.

The Two Second Rule

What is the two second rule? It is a simple method of keeping a safe distance between you and the vehicle in front, at any speed. The importance of separation distances has been explained throughout this book, and they should be remembered at all times. As a basic reminder; on the open road, one yard for every one mile per hour should be maintained — so a car travelling on a dry road at 50mph should have a gap of 50yd from the vehicle in front. As the speed increase so does the distance from the vehicle in front. As a guide, when driving in built-up areas at a speed below 20mph a minimum distance of one foot for every one mile per hour should be allowed. As the vehicle leaves the built-up area and the road speed increases, so must the distance from the vehicle in front. Horrific accidents have occurred because all the drivers involved thought they could stop in time; they didn't. There are many drivers today who wish they had kept a safe distance from the vehicle in front.

At night, in built-up areas where visibility is poor, dipped headlamps should be used so that the driver's view is extended and other road users can see his vehicle more easily. A distance should be maintained so that the light from the dipped headlamps do not dazzle the driver in front. The headlamps must be correctly set so as to provide maximum illumination of the road without causing other drivers to be dazzled.

One essential fact to be remembered when driving at any time is that the driver should always be in a position to stop his vehicle well within the distance he can see to be clear. At night the driver's view is restricted more when it is raining, therefore speed should be reduced and the following distance from the vehicle in front extended.

The Two-Second Rule

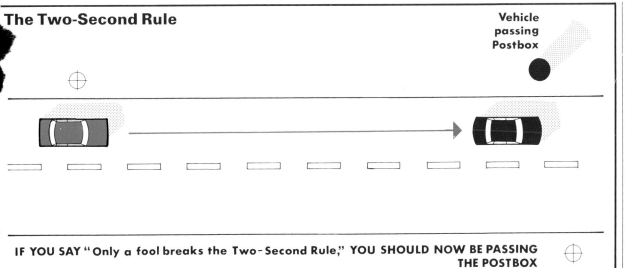

Vehicle passing Postbox

IF YOU SAY "Only a fool breaks the Two-Second Rule," YOU SHOULD NOW BE PASSING THE POSTBOX

Far left below:
This sign in Berkshire warns drivers that they are following too closely to each other. Not many drivers take advantage of the advice given.

Below:
Much has been written about the following distance from the vehicle in front. When passing or overtaking a cyclist or motorcyclist, adequate space must be given to them, because they are exposed to the elements, and you are not.

Passing Thought

Whenever you are driving on the road and you find yourself in a position such that you have to swerve or brake hard to avoid another road user, pause before you blame the other driver. Rather, consider whether you should have been there, and what would have happened if you had been going at twice the speed!

BICYCLE.   BRUISER.

11. General Advice